PATTERN INTERRUPT

by DARREN STOTT

Supernaturalist Ministries & Publications

Newcastle, Washington

Published by Supernaturalist Ministries & Publications

8011 128th AVE SE

Newcastle, WA. 98056

www.iSupernaturalist.com

ISBN: 978-0-692-75741-3

In Loving Memory of

Darrel Edwin Stott

5/3/1948 - 7/6/2016

CONTENTS

A FIRST LOOK AT PATTERN INTERRUPT

Chapter 1

Welcome to the Garden: *Understanding Why We Hide*

You are not alone. The problem is bigger than you. It's called the human condition and it affects us all to this day. The Garden is where it all began and it is here where we discover the methodology behind the madness. You will learn how to interrupt fear-based patterns that produce shame. You will be challenged to embrace a new covering and a new kind of hiddenness.

Chapter 2

Puppet Masters: *Breaking the Pattern of Manipulation and Control*

Biblically, the only person you have permission to control is yourself. In fact, self-control is one of the fruits of the Spirit seen in Galatians 5:23. You will discover the motivational structure behind manipulation and you will learn the most common patterns of control and how to get free.

Chapter 3

Who Told You That: *Discerning the Difference between Facts and Truth*

Most my life I believed I was bad at sports until just recently when the Lord asked me where I got that fact. The truth wasn't that I was bad at sports; I just lacked the discipline needed in order to excel. Recent research shows that talent is overrated. Our genes don't make us great. Applying ourselves with intentionality is what can set us apart. Most people believe that facts equal truths; however, we will dispel that myth. You will be given permission to shine in areas you never thought possible.

Chapter 4

The Winepress is for Winemaking: *Dismantling Defeat*

Gideon was afraid, hiding, and found himself threshing wheat in a winepress. Abraham was frustrated, depressed and childless. He and his wife were in the process of writing their servant into their will. All they wanted was a child. A generation longs for the good news of the gospel and a redemptive power that can change everything. Gideon became a warrior, Abraham became a father, and you are about to step into a new realm of courage.

Chapter 5

Tap Dancing For Jesus: *Why We Do the Silly Things We Do*

Many drive themselves silly, engaging in outrageous behaviors that end up resulting in burn out. Too many new Christians throw in the towel because they are trying to earn acceptance from God, as well as people. Many people wrestle with temptation and secret sin and can't figure out how to get free. Behavior is never random. It is the outcome of our expectations. In this chapter we will study the motivational factors behind sinful and self-righteous behaviors.

Chapter 6

The Rumblers: *New Breed, Pattern Interrupters*

The shaking isn't random. Intercessors have been sowing into this very day for generations. Heaven is being released onto the earth through a new breed of pattern interrupters or what I refer to as *rumblers*. There is wave of revivalist that are emerging and they don't look anything like they did in the past. They aren't just screaming in microphones at revival conferences. They are everywhere. They are the ones teaching your children, making your mocha, fixing your teeth, legislating in Congress and legislating in the Heavens.

Chapter 7

The Presence Driven Life: *The Secret to Liberation*

There is a shift in the church taking us from being driven by Christian purposes to being driven into Christ Himself. Under the old model our efficiency was determined by the fruit of processes, but under the new model our efficiency will be determined by our level of trust and rest in Him. We have gravely understated the importance and value of His presence within the Church and our lives, but He is coming to remedy that.

Chapter 8

I'm Sorry You're Going to Have to Leave: *Displacing the Demonic*

When we partner with rejection, isolation, and abandonment we are actually cohabitating with demons; demons who expect cream in their coffee every morning. Learn how to break alliances with demonic influence and evict hell from your life forever.

Chapter 9

Reframe the Future: *The Power of the Word of God*

The leading cause of death in America is heart disease and isn't it interesting that hope deferred is what makes the heart sick? Promising hope sells books, pharmaceuticals, and even wins elections. The world has become frustrated because the usual suspects have not delivered on their promise. The good news is that Christ Jesus is the hope of glory. The Living Word, the spirit of Christ Jesus is about to manifest through the body of Christ in a fresh way. The prophetic, as we have known it, is in a season of shifting. The Bride of Christ is about to begin reframing the future through the power of the spoken Word of God. The Heralds of Hope are about to be released.

Chapter 10
Green Light: *Now Go!*

Every encounter with God in the Bible leads to one word, "Go." Perhaps you've been waiting at the same intersection for decades. Good news, you have the green light. Now is the time to move.

SNEEZE!

An Introduction

WHAT IS A PATTERN INTERRUPT?

I sat at the kitchen table with beads of sweat sledding down my forehead. I was being trained to sell insurance, a venture that would be short-lived. I, along with my trainer, Wade, were insurance salesmen and we sat across the table from a couple that was actively weighing their options. It was the summit of the presentation and our pitch was done. Wade waited with his Montblanc fountain pen twitching in his hand. It hovered over an application and he gently nudged Mr. Rosemond with a question.

"Okay, what's your social security number?"

The couple thumbed through the documents and brochures. The wife looked at her husband as if urging him to answer the question. The retired Boeing engineer scowled. Obviously he had not woken up that morning with an overwhelming desire to purchase more insurance. We waited. Leaning into the tension, that cold and awkward silence. Then Mr. Rosemond responded, "Gentlemen, thank you for your time but…"

Just then a loud and embarrassing sneeze exploded from Wade's face. Mrs. Rosemond lunged for the Kleenex box. Wade screamed in horror. Mr. Rosemond acted like a young medic again on the fields of war. He lunged to Wade's aid. The chaos lasted just for a moment and when the fog lifted Wade began telling stories and giving more examples, explaining how the policy had helped other couples. It was as we had gone back in time to the beginning of the appointment. This time the couple sat with a new level of empathy. Wade was no longer a salesman. He was now a sneeze survivor. Wade wrote up the policy. He made the sale. As we drove off in Wade's luxurious car I decided to state the obvious, "Mr. Rosemond wasn't going to purchase that policy. How did you change his mind?"

"I didn't." Wade replied, "He changed his own mind."

"But he was going to tell you 'no'."

"'No'- was his programmed default response. I had to turn off his auto-pilot so he could make the best decision possible."

Wade had a smirk on his face. He knew something that I didn't.

"The sneeze, Darren, it wasn't real."

I was confused. A fake sneeze?

"It was a pattern interrupt."

He was no longer a salesman. He was now a Jedi Master and I was his young padawan.

"Mr. Rosemond was going to say 'no' because that's what he's been conditioned to say to every opportunity that is offered to him. I saw the 'no' coming and I waited for it, and right when he was about to shoot down the opportunity, I sneezed. The sneeze was an event that jarred him out of the same ol' same ol' pattern."

I wondered. Had this 2001 Mercedes CL600 been paid-in-full by fake sneezes? I decided then and there that I didn't like fake sneezes.

This book is all about pattern interrupts: events that jar us out of our preconditioned and defeater responses or patterns. This book is the sneeze, but it's not fake nor manipulative. You are getting full-disclosure right here. This book exists to help you dismantle defeat, overcome ordinary and become a rumbler by exposing the enemy's methodology behind mediocrity.

WHO IS THIS BOOK FOR?

Humans.

Insecurity, regret and shame-based control is part of the human condition. When Adam and Eve sinned against God, a foreign and toxic ingredient called fear entered into the default dynamic of the soul.

This book begins by looking at why we try to cover ourselves and hide. We will look at the original sin that framed patterns of defeat and God's perfect pattern interrupt that would change everything. As you read this book, you will hear God walking through your garden. You will sense his sweet fatherly presence summoning you to come out of hiding and to come into your place of true identity as a covenant son.

This book is for people who battle with chaos, anxiety, stress and busyness. This book is for those who can't seem to catch their breath, let alone free up the bandwidth needed to be obedient to the Lord. This book is for those who need the Holy Spirit to hover into their void and bring peace.

This is a book for those who are wrapped in leaves, hiding behind trees, getting stung by bees and wanting to sneeze, but can't because the sound might give up their location to a God who is quickly approaching. In this book I will encourage you to sneeze. To be found by your creator and King.

This book will help you discover that God has called you for such a time as this. You will be invited to come out from hiding and partner with the spirit of hope, which is the spirit of Christ Jesus himself. The Lord is preparing a stage for you to make his Name known.

I want to make a commitment to you. I commit to be a pattern interrupt. I commit to do my best to jar you out of your ordinary routine. With God's help, I will partner with the Holy to drag you out of your cave kicking and screaming. I desperately want to expose you as the forgiven Christ man/woman that Jesus says you are.

I'm not a big fan of male cheerleaders and yet that's kind of what God has called me to be. I am here to cheer you on. You are going to do some amazing things for the Kingdom of God and it all starts here, right now, with you.

HOW DOES THIS BOOK WORK?

- Directives

  - Each chapter of this book ends with three directives (three things that the reader is encouraged to immediately begin doing or stop doing). Directives are simply action items that assist the reader in developing new habits.

- Small Group Discussion Questions

  - Each chapter ends with small group discussion questions. Life-change rarely occurs in isolation. Within the context of community, this book could fuel a revolution of action and release the kind of faith that inspires radical Kingdom works. Bust this book out in your small group and get ready to go deep.

- Activation

  - Each chapter ends with an activation prayer. Read these prayers over yourself and expect the Lord to shift you from ordinary to extraordinary.

SNEEZE

My kids don't really understand the game Hide-And-Go-Seek. For them being found is the best part. I count and they all run and hide. When I am searching for them I declare loudly throughout the house, "Here I come. I am going to find you, and when I find you, I am going to tickle you!"

When I get close to where they are hiding they will usually do something, like fake a sneeze. They do it on purpose because they want to be found by me. I always fulfill my promise. I grab them and I tickle them because that's what daddies do with their children.

Many people hide from God and people because they are scared of what will happen when they are found. Your fear of punishment is about to be washed away. You soon will have enough courage to fake a sneeze, on purpose, so that your Father finds you. Guess what? When He finds you, He's going to tickle you.

Go ahead and sneeze.

1
WELCOME TO THE GARDEN

Understanding Why We Hide

"I heard the sound of you in the garden, and I was afraid, because I was naked, and I hid myself."

- Genesis 3:10

DESPICABLE ME

"Yup, my dad knows the President of the United States," I said confidently. I believed it. "He talks to the president on the telephone all the time. He even led the president into a relationship with Jesus."

There I was. An eight-year-old, skinny boy with my big melon head covered in crazy, curly, brownish hair. I was lying for no apparent reason and they were eating it up. Our recently converted neighbors lived across the street and were now attending our church. Now all five of them sat and listened as I explained why my dad was cooler than Billy Graham.

Our church had recently participated in a Billy Graham crusade and these neighbors couldn't stop talking about it, and the more they talked, the more jealous I became. They obviously had too high of an opinion of Billy Graham and I was going to have to remedy that.

It was all good-in-the-hood until the phone rang. It was our neighbors. They wanted to fact check my story. Had Darrel, their neighbor, and my (rock star) dad really led President George Herbert Walker Bush in the sinner's prayer? They wanted to know more.

"He said what?" my mom looked horrified.

I didn't look up. I knew what was happening. I tried to eat but my hand was shaking. I put down my fork, and looked over at my dad. He had no idea what was going on, nor did he realize how significant I had made him. My mom was about to ruin it. I was about to get in big trouble; like, spanking-level trouble.

"I'm so sorry. I don't know why he said that. I'm going to talk to him right now. We'll be calling you back in just a moment."

Moments later I was on the phone apologizing for lying. All five members of their family were on the phone at the same time, and what made it worse was that my apology wasn't enough. They wanted to know why I lied. Don't you just hate it when people want to understand your motive for sinning? I honestly didn't have the wisdom necessary to explain myself. The truth was that I lied, just to lie (never a good sign for a pastor's kid). I was busted and embarrassed, and I had to own it.

Where did I learn this behavior? I had just partnered with the spirit of jealousy and defamed Billy Graham by making up a stupid lie. Despite the 1980's Christian propaganda movies warning parents of the perils of comic books, ACDC and the Smurfs, I can assure you that this behavior wasn't learned from an outside influence. It was inherent. I, by nature, was born with less-than-perfect DNA that traces back to our first less-than-perfect parents, Adam and Eve. Like me, they had "an incident," a mistake that would reframe humanity's identity as despicable by nature from that point forward.

In Genesis 3, Satan takes on the form of a crafty serpent and entices Adam and Eve into making a choice to distrust and disobey God. Engaging with this deception led to an outbreak of generational patterns that manifested in brokenness, bondage, and death.

All of humanity, by default, has been born with a flawed record, into patterns of chaos and anarchy. All of humanity is in desperate need of a true Savior - a Savior with the power to intervene and save us from our individual and generational pattern loops.

FROM BUMMED TO BITTER

My dad and his dad were both pastors and I swore I would not be the third generation pastor. I cursed the concept and yet God in his perfect timing and process called me and prepared me unknowingly. The three of us would pastor the same church, at different times, with different names and yet the same church nevertheless. This church was a big deal to me. In fact, it was the core of my identity. It was my castle, and I was royalty. So when my parents got divorced and the new pastors took over, I felt like Ronald McDonald trying to say goodbye to McDonalds...forever. For the first time in my life, my mom and I began church shopping. Unfortunately you can't buy a new church at Costco.

I was broken. I had more questions than answers. I began my junior year at a new school, trying to make new friends, which bummed me out. My junior year was a year of brokenness and yet I was smart enough to know that depressed kids don't usually make for a good Homecoming King, so I branded myself as the creative (and might I add good-looking) class clown. I was "the funny guy." That was my covering, but more on that later.

By my senior year of high school, every shred of brokenness was gone. It had been left to mold within my wellspring of life. My heart was now contaminated. I had transitioned from bummed-out to bitter. There's something about bitterness: it has this sneaky way of ascribing self-worth by devaluing and reducing others. The more judgmental I became of Christians and the church, the more self-righteous I felt. I hadn't realized it but my bitterness had blinded me. I was as blind as a fruit bat and whenever people would try to get me to see, I'd include them into the group of people that I hated. I thought I knew every problem with the Church and I took it on myself to educate others. My heart posture set the stage for a series of self-justified life patterns that were unhealthy and sinful. I felt vindicated in my lifestyle choices because I was able to successfully judge anyone who said I was wrong.

I had a belief, "Your private sin justifies my obvious sin."

Rather than trusting the Lord with my disappointments, I took control. My rebellion was my preference for escape. I was able to hide the real me behind an angry me.

NO LONGER VIKINGS

It was the respected theologian, author, and pope-of-evangelicals, John Stott, who told my Grandfather of our vicious Viking roots. Stotts had a legacy of sheep stealing, womanizing, and brawling. If your ancestors' European village was pillaged between the eighth and eleventh century, it was probably us. Sorry.

My Grandpa was a first-generation Christian given the grace to break out of the pub-crawling, hatred-driven, self-destructive patterns that claimed the lives of so many Stotts before him. His victories were extraordinary because many of them were with generational giants, demonic villains given legal jurisdiction to taunt, haunt and influence without restraint. I honor my Grandpa, not because he was perfect, but rather because he embraced God's grace as his weapon of choice. It was his slingshot. I believe that my Grandpa died an overcomer. At the age of 92, he lived longer than his father and grandfathers before him. The day he died, he led a woman to the Lord. She said, "He was dying and yet he wasn't concerned about himself. He was concerned about me."

We are no longer Vikings, sheep stealers, womanizers, brawlers, and hatred-driven men. We are now lovers of God. The blood of Jesus was and is actively redefining the identity of our surname. My father traveled the globe, spending most of his time in Indonesia, Russia and the Ukraine, encouraging people in the Lord and spreading revival fire. He has had his own battles and I have had mine, and these battles are extraordinary. We are getting to defeat the giants that my grandpa didn't. We are clearing the land of the enemy so our grandchildren can live in peace.

Remember, the temptations you face are not unique to you. The patterns that you have fallen into may well be generational. Your dad probably felt the same pressure that you feel now. There are Goliaths that tormented your family-line for generations and now you are the David that is going to slay them.

WHY HUMANS HIDE

After Adam and Eve sinned they realized that their sin had cost them their covering. Not only were they naked but somebody was coming for them. God, Himself was in the garden and was calling their names. They could hear the sticks breaking under His feet. He was close. And for the first time in their lives, they experienced fear.

From that day forward, fear would influence the natural disposition of the human heart resulting in habitual hiding. It is because of fear that we hide from God, from ourselves and from others. We'll hide behind anything: our jobs, our addictions, our families, and even our religious duties.

When I was a kid, I hated *The Wizard of Oz*. It freaked me right out and kept me from sleeping for several nights. Despite my childhood trauma, the cowardly lion who couldn't roar fascinated me. In the story, the lion wanted one thing from the wizard, the gift of courage. Isn't it interesting? We have been created in the image and likeness of the Lion of Judah and yet in the garden we lost our courage, and fear came and robbed our roar.

Just before taking His last breath, Jesus roared. After pleading for the mercy of God on behalf of humanity, He declared once and for all, "It is finished."

Just like that, the silence ended. The veil in the temple was torn and the era of separation was over. Sinful men would now have access to a holy God through the son, Jesus Christ. The spirit of adoption was released onto the earth and now man has a true and perfect covering, the blood of Jesus.

By default, humans hide. By nature we are naked, uncovered, ashamed, and scared. Many believers ride the emotional roller coaster of fear - up and down, up and down – stuck in a field of apathy while tearing off dandelion petals and reciting, "He loves me. He loves me not."

Humans hide because of fear. But what if you didn't have to be afraid anymore?

Adam and Eve's fear and shame led to the logical action of trying to take control. They immediately went to work, making loincloths out of leaves to hide their nakedness, but hiding their nakedness wasn't enough. When they heard God coming through the garden, they went all the way and literally hid themselves as well.

UPGRADE

There's a clothing store in New York called Alexander McQueen. A visit to this store will cost you $1,847, making it one of the most expensive clothing stores in the United States of America. A man's pajama set costs $715, and if you are paying the cost of admission then you best be leaving with more than just a pair of jammies.

Imagine that your entire wardrobe consisted of an exclusive K-Mart collection with a total value of $100, and Jesus called you up and invited you to go shopping at Alexander McQueen, all expenses paid. What would you say? This is what the Lord does in Genesis 3:21. He says, "Guys, what on earth are you wearing?"

"Oh, yea, um this?" Adam points down at his groin while blushing, "This is 100% organic fig leaf that we sewed together."

"That I sewed together!" Eve interrupts boldly.

God says, "I still love you guys, and I still want to cover you, but everything is going to be completely different now."

Adam and Eve, in their own striving, attempted to cover their shame and nakedness, but after being confronted by God, He in His mercy covered them with *kĕthoneth*, the Hebrew word for garments, and the same word that would be used repeatedly throughout the Old Testament for priestly garments. Right then and there, God, the designer of designers, made them perfectly crafted tunics of skin. How would you like to have clothing that was made by God? This really isn't about clothing at all. This was a prophetic drama, a physical foretelling of a true and perfect spiritual covering that would manifest through the blood of His Son.

Adam and Eve didn't have to assume their own lordship. Even though they had sinned against God, He still loved them and wanted to provide for them.

HEALING HAPPENS

I had been expecting this call, and here it was. The phone rang and after picking up the receive, I heard her voice, "Hi, darling!"

It was our family friend, and Elder of my church, the church that we left, the church that was renamed "New Beginnings" (because whenever something bad happens in a church they always change the name to New Beginnings). Gail Fleming, had just returned from Australia where she was itinerating and helping to facilitate a youth revival. Apparently she had heard from God about returning to New Beginnings and resurrecting Seattle Revival Center, and now she wanted to meet with me. I didn't want to meet with her, but out of respect I agreed to an appointment.

I sat in Gail's office (formally my dad's office). She sat near me, smiling, and then she politely asked me a question that she already knew the answer to, "How are you doing, honey?"

She was more familiar with brokenness that I had ever been. She had a relationship with Jesus that had been forged by fire. A few years prior, her husband had left her, and instead of growing bitter, she grew better. She handled her disappointments better than me. She never dumped her sorrows like seed on the side of the road, she planted her tears like a farmer and now she was reaping sheaves of joy.

"I'm fine," I lied trying to smile. My toes were curled up in my shoes. The side of my mouth was twitching uncontrollably.

"Darren, I wanted to meet with you to tell you that I'm sorry." She was sincere and it was weirding me out.

"Sorry for what?"

"I'm sorry for everything," and she continued apologizing, on and on, for stuff she didn't do. It was heartfelt, it was comforting, and it was confusing.

"But you didn't do any of these things, so why are you apologizing?"

She paused and stared right at me with determination, "Because someone needs to."

She was standing in the gap. The door of my heart was starting to open. I didn't want it to. I thought I had locked it. I didn't want to be there. I didn't want to forgive people. I wasn't ready for any pattern interrupts, at least not right now. My hurt, after all, was my excuse for my careless choices. If I started forgiving people, what license to sin would I have left? I chose to be polite and I forgave her, but I didn't realize the power of forgiveness as the words slipped right through my lips, "I forgive you."

I had been set up without knowing it. God walked into my garden and found me in my hiding place. A seed of hope was planted in my heart. God was about to hijack my course. It would not be a quick process but nevertheless it was inevitable. God's plan would not be voided by sin. His blood would ruthlessly cover, redeem, and restore.

I later had a dream that I was back at my church leading worship and singing a song I had never heard before. When I woke up, I was still singing the song, and when I stopped singing, it was gone. The seed had germinated. God used a dream to put desire in my heart to return to my church. It wasn't but a short period of time and I found myself back at Seattle Revival Center, leading worship, and needless to say, there were many moments that played out exactly as I witnessed in my dream. God didn't tease me with what could be. He gave me hope, and then He satisfied it by allowing my dream to come true. His love brought me out of hiding.

BREAKTHROUGH

What mistakes have you made? Where is there shame and where are you inserting your control in hopes of achieving your desired outcomes? At this moment, take time to realize how lousy of a god you are. Honor yourself by being honest with yourself. Take this moment to slow down. You don't need to read 700 words per minute right now. Your heart is trying to tell you something.

I know from experience that there is nothing more terrifying than engaging with hope. After living with disappointment for such a long time, we frame our lives so that silly things excite us and heavenly things annoy us. It's easier for us to discredit hope because then we don't have to worry about being let down. I get it. Life has let you down. People have let you down. You've let yourself down. And yet I must tell you this simple truth, "God is good and His mercy endures forever!" This is your time to come out of hiding. God wants to upgrade your wardrobe. There's been a breakthrough that's been ordered for you.

This is your time.

This is your year.

This is your moment to rise and shine.

He never called you to be ordinary. He called you to reveal His extraordinary character and nature. He called you to manifest His authority and power. He called you to defy the odds and make impossibilities blush. You aren't a cowardly lion. You are a son of a terrifying lion. You never lost your roar. You've just never had a reason to let it rip. This is your season of breakthrough. Jesus is taking you shopping for some new clothes. It's time for breakthrough. It's time to roar.

3 DIRECTIVES:

- Identify – the source(s) of your shame. Write them out in a journal. Go back and begin to process the factors involved in your "worst" sins. Ask yourself, "Why did I try to reduce Billy Graham and elevate my own father above him?" :-)

- Share – those things you have never shared. Secrets consume bandwidth and a lack of bandwidth is a lack of vitality and creativity. Remember, honesty is the highest form of honor. The highest form of striving is lying. Work less and share more.

- Cut the strings – to those who you have tried to control and manipulate. Apologize to those you have attempted to control. Be specific, use examples, and explain the motivation and fears behind your actions. Your honesty will forge a deeper place of intimacy.

SMALL GROUP DISCUSSION QUESTIONS:

- Have you ever felt pressure to hide the real you? If so, how did that pressure manifest?

- Without dishonoring the people God has called you to be family with, share the patterns you have seen in your family line that you would love to have broken.

- Adam and Eve hid behind fig leaves. What things have you been tempted to hide behind?

ACTIVATION:

Declare it – Spend 20 minutes each day with the Lord. Ready, study and declare these scriptures over your life.

Sunday – Wednesday:

- 2 Corinthians 5:17
- Galatians 2:20
- Isaiah 43:18

Thursday – Saturday:

- Colossians 3:9-10
- 2 Corinthians 5:17-21
- Ezekiel 11:19-20

Live it - Share with your closest friends and family this new journey. Share your findings. Share your hopes for this present season and invite them to be a part.

WORKSHEET:

- My sin: _____
- Areas of shame:_____
- How I've hidden as a result: _____

2
PUPPET MASTERS

Breaking the Pattern of Manipulation and Control

"There is no fear in love, but perfect love casts out fear. For fear has to do with punishment."

– 1 John 4:18

PARTNERING WITH REBELLION

I was rummaging through artifacts on my mom's desk in search of a highlighter or something when I found an email that had been printed. It was from Gail to the elders. She stated that she felt God was calling her to come back from Australia and pastor, rebuild, and get the church ready for a harvest. I pondered these things in my heart until the following Sunday when I would erupt with uninvited thoughts on the matter.

I had just grabbed a second helping of powdered mashed potatoes, macaroni and cheese and chocolate milk from our favorite Sunday-afternoon buffet. I sat down at the table, joining my mom, and John and Connye Scheda, who were elders at the church.

"I hear Gail's coming back?" Connye ate a bite of macaroni and cheese. We both were fond of macaroni and cheese.

"We'll see." John answered, quickly swerving around the topic like a motorbike around a stalled car on the freeway.

"So, it's kind of interesting," I continued, "My mom and I have been going to all these different churches, and I've noticed something: the churches that are successful have these pastors that carry this *thing*. I can't explain it. It's this *thing*. They walk out on the stage, and everybody's like, 'Whoa! that's the pastor!' A pastor has to have that *thing*. Gail... doesn't have that *thing*. Yea, sure the church needs a new pastor and stuff, but a woman? Do you really think that's going to work?"

I don't remember their response. I was too self-absorbed. I had a big swig of chocolate milk.

As I blasted away at the church, friends and religion; I took control. My new friend was the spirit of rebellion. He became my covering and he was even kind enough to allow me to worship myself. The weird thing is, I actually cared about the church and Gail, but I was too scared to entertain hope. It was easier to attack the people that I loved than it was to actually believe again.

1 Samuel 15:23 reveals that rebellion is as the sin of witchcraft. We tend to not take that scripture seriously, but it's true. Rebellion is a fungus. It's subtle, self-seeking, subversive and totally destructive. As time went on, I became the very thing that I hated. I judged and attempted to control judgmental and controlling people. The irony: I was becoming my own enemy.

It's time to confess. I wasn't ultimately a victim of controlling people. I was a controller myself. So speaking from experience, let me say that control is never the problem in-and-of-itself. It's just a symptom. In order to achieve aesthetic gain, weeds can be hacked instead of pulled, but underneath the hard soil there is a mature root structure that will surely break through the surface again. A hard heart can act like hardened soil and actually protect a root of bitterness. In order for control to be pulled, the wounded heart must become saturated and soft. This process of saturation takes grace and time, but be assured there is hope for controlling people. I'm proof that breakthrough is possible.

John 10 tells us what to expect when we put our trust in other false shepherds. Jesus says "the thief comes to steal kill and destroy," and I can testify that this is no lie. I partnered with the spirit of rebellion and he turned out to be a thief. Rebelling was my way of keeping people away from my broken heart. By taking control, I could hide in plain sight.

HOW TO IDENTIFY REBELLION?

The problem with deception is that no one actually knows when they've been deceived. It is likely you probably have no idea if you are rebellious, controlling or manipulative. So how do you identify rebellion in your own life?

1. Remember

    - Search your memory banks for what people have told you in the past.

    - Have you ever been accused of being rebellious, controlling or manipulative? Did you pass it off as nonsense?

- Before you go in search of new information take inventory of the old information.

2. Ask

- Ask the question, "What do you see in me?"

- Seek uncensored feedback (from people who don't lie). Be specific in your questioning, and show gratitude to those who have the courage to level with you.

3. Surrender

- Surrender your lordship by giving up your control rights.

- Develop a servant plan.

- Find new ways to contribute your time, effort, passion and finances without having to be in charge.

- Find the fun in making others look good and don't forget that the end does not justify the means.

- Sin is sin. Commit to stop justifying your behavior.

PATTERNS OF CONTROL

Imagine you're a cowboy. You have shaggy brown hair and a ridiculous cowboy hat. Your unmaintained mustache covers your mouth, and Marlboro covers your B.O. You're on a stagecoach, flying down the side of a mountain. You're screaming. Two horses are partnering with gravity to get you from point A to B as quickly as possible, even if it kills you. In your hands you hold the reins but they're not connected to the horses' mouths. You will need to climb out onto each horse and place the bits in each of their mouths while trying not to die. Take a snapshot of this in your mind. This is a picture of the human condition. Sin puts us in a ruthless predicament and despite impossible factors we attempt to regain control of our own lives by engaging in mere stupidity. Hence the need for a pattern interrupt.

We don't wrestle with horses. We wrestle with people. Despite princes and powers, most of our wrestling is with flesh and blood. When our stagecoach is out of control we usually try to find the two people we can blame and attempt to get bits into their mouths. The lie that many people believe is that if we can control people then we can achieve our most desirable outcome. Control and manipulation, like rebellion, is demonic and rooted in sorcery. Rebellion is a form of control, but control isn't limited to just rebellion. There are many other manifestations of control that are unfortunately far too common.

DO YOU SWEAR?

There's something about swearing. Four letter words immediately arrest atmospheres. A swear word can be more frightening than a gunshot and is often used in the same fashion. A swear word can end a conversation, a relationship, and even a marriage. A swear word is like a loaded nine-millimeter in that it can be used to hold others hostage. Swearing can be a form of verbal control. If nothing else, it can be a window into the state of one's heart. If swearing is a common part of your verbal diet, it's time for a pattern interrupt.

CAN YOU HEAR ME NOW?

There are appropriate applications for yelling, such as motivating soldiers or intercessors at a prayer rally, singing in a metal band, or expressing fear on a roller coaster. God created yelling so that communication could be possible when there's physical distance. The problem is that many subconsciously engage in yelling not because of physical distance but because of emotional distance. It's an indication light, like on a car's dashboard, a warning that there is distance between the hearts of the two parties. Not only is yelling an indicator of the heart and emotional distance but many times it's actually a form of verbal control. The reason why it works is because it's a pattern interrupt. It snaps the brain out of autopilot, temporarily paralyzing the other party, and because it works, people do it. If we use volume to control people, then we are engaging with a spirit of manipulation. These behaviors are typically not one-time occurrences. They are learned behaviors that become practiced patterns. If your love language involves yelling, you need a pattern interrupt.

HIDING BEHIND HUMOR

On December 18th, 1997 actor, comedian, and Saturday Night Live star, Chris Farley died of a drug overdose at the age of 33. It was a bizarre mimicking of his role model, John Belushi, who also was a SNL cast member, who struggled with a drug and alcohol addiction and died at the age of 33.

Bill Hicks, Greg Giraldo, Sam Kinison (a former preacher) and Robin Williams are some of the most gifted and hilarious people who ever walked this planet. These are men who all died prematurely and had an ability to hide behind their humor.

Comedy can be a form of control. Quick wit name-calling, mockery, and even just simply acting silly in order to get a laugh can be used as a manipulative tool to gain a certain outcome. I recall a story told by Pastor Craig Groeschel at LifeChurch.TV in which he was talking about how the Lord called him into a season where he completely removed humor from his preaching. The Lord told him that he was basically hiding behind his humor. Today Craig is just as hilarious as ever but he's also radically transparent and effective in ministry. The Lord had to balance him out with a pattern interrupt.

ARE YOU SAD?

Are you known for emotional breakdowns, fits of rage, silent treatment, subtle or quiet weeping? Although these behaviors can be symptoms for psychological and chemical imbalances, they can also be manifestations of control instigated in order to achieve an outcome. I'm not trying to give you ammo to fire on someone else. The question we must ask is if we ourselves are engaging in these activities in order to get our own way? Perhaps you don't need medication or another evaluation. It could be that these behaviors have become habitual because they bring about a sense of temporary peace by which you can breathe, function and carry out your life's activities without interference from others. If so, it's time for a pattern interrupt. If you lack total self-control over your emotions, it's probably time to schedule an appointment to meet with your pastor and doctor.

ECONOMIC ABUSE

Money symbolically represents power and freedom. Through the withholding of money, one can actually treat another as a functional slave. Economic control is a tolerated and accepted form of abuse within many Christian relationships and marriages that involves withholding or offering finances in order to achieve a desired outcome. One party simply withholds money from the other, sometimes opens up other bank accounts that the spouse has no access to and then offers money if and when a desired performance is achieved. The controller often prohibits the other from making money, spending money, or even asking probing questions about money. Economic control often involves shaming another for how they've saved or spent their money.

Jesus said how we view money reveals the practical condition and state of your heart. If we are partnering with financial shame and fear, then economic control is inevitable.

Are you using finances to control another person? If so, stop it. Consider this a sneeze moment (see the introduction) and please take your time in the activation at the end of this chapter.

SEX

Sexual control involves attaining a desired outcome by manipulating another by offering or withholding sexual satisfaction. Sex is an act of worship that was created to take place within the confines of covenant marriage. It is a sacred, soul-tying/bonding act that reveals transparency, vulnerability, and beauty like no other activity. Sex is a prophetic drama that testifies of the oneness and union possible between the bride of Christ and the bridegroom. It is for pleasure and procreation. Love creates. Isn't it like the devil to turn sex into an act of manipulation and control?

1 Corinthians 7:5 says "Do not deprive one another (sexually), except perhaps by agreement for a limited time, that you may devote yourselves to prayer; but then come together again (sexually), so that Satan may not tempt you because of your lack of self-control."

Sexual deprivation within marriage is acceptable if it's been agreed upon by both parties in order to pursue closer intimacy with the Lord, but I'd say if you're going to fast, fast food first.

Sex is a gift. Don't withhold it so you can achieve a desired outcome.

PHYSICAL ABUSE

Have you ever physically abused someone? Have you ever been physically abused? If so, keep reading. There is healing available for you. Jesus can be your perfect and beautiful pattern interrupt. If you've never been involved in physical abuse you may be surprised to hear that this issue is just as common within the church as it is outside.

Physical abuse is a form of control that aims to physically do whatever is necessary to achieve a desired outcome. It can involve standing over someone, blocking a doorway, hitting, threatening to harm another, throwing objects, driving recklessly, cutting, pulling hair, tying or confining another, and preventing someone from seeking medical care.

Fear and shame are factors that create atmospheres where abuse occurs. The Church has tolerated fear and shame for such a long time that we have created churches where abuse can hide and patterns can remain and continue underneath the disguise of religion. Typically, when physical abuse occurs within a church, the abusive spouse is reported and the victim is received and is slowly nursed back to health. In some tragic cases, the abuser is actually embraced and the victim is rejected and even blamed for instigating the abuse.

In the scriptures, God goes to great length to identify Himself with the poor, needy, afflicted and abused, however He also shows great concern for the prisoner. We have an obligation to do justice, yes, but we must also have a commandment to love mercy. We, the church, must become a safe place - for those who lash out in anger and control - to confess their sin and to begin a process of recovery and restoration. The church has said that it's the justice system's job to punish and rehabilitate physical abusers and, for the most part, we have washed our hands of those who walk in this pattern. Because of our history of ignorance and punishment-based cultures, those who are in sin typically hide in the church until their sins find them out.

Pastor and author Danny Silk was once told, "You're the pastor of the church with all the child abusers." Danny replied, "No, we're the church where child abusers can't hide."

At the end of this chapter, I will provide several resources for those who are victims of physical abuse and those who have attempted to control others by inserting physical force. Your freedom is of utmost concern to the Lord.

RELIGIOUS CONTROL

In the New York Times best seller, *Freakonomics*, economists Steven Levitt and Stephen J. Dubner expose the cheating scandal within Japan's sumo wrestling scene. What made this such a shocking revelation is that nobody ever expected cheating to be taking place within such an ancient, stoic, and honored sport. It was almost as if

Sumo wrestling was above such an allegation. It took some serious mathematical number crunching in order to expose the scandal. The same could be said of the Roman Catholic Church and the sex scandal and endless allegations and investigations that began to explode in the early 2000's. Often times control and manipulation exist in the places where you least expect it. Hyper religious atmospheres are greenhouses for control. Religion has a way of creating a façade by which sin can hide.

Religious control is exactly that: it's an attempt to use religion, religious guilt, condemning tones, and even quoting scripture verses in order to strong-arm another into a specific performance-based lifestyle.

Phrases are used like, "You can't divorce me, God hates divorce," or "Woman, the Bible says you must submit to me."

It's important to remember Matthew 22:36-40, that says that all the laws and the prophets hinge upon one commandment, the great commandment, love God with everything we are and love others as we love ourselves. Christianity in its truest form is not a religion. It's a tribe of Christ lovers. Jesus prayed in John 17 that we would actually be known as Christians by our love. This is where the contrast exists: religion demands performance whereas relationship makes room for love.

The Bible was not given to us so we could preach at people. It was given to us to reveal the character and nature of God. Someone once said, "The Bible is God's love letter to His children. If you don't know you're loved, it's because you've been reading someone else's mail."

Religious behavior is control-based; it attempts to convince us that we have to say, do, and think the right thing in order to be accepted. But, if we know that Christ was rejected so that we could be infinitely accepted, then we don't have to perform for love. You live from love.

CUT THE STRINGS

Pinocchio was a lifeless wooden puppet that could be skillfully manipulated by his humble and loving creator, Geppetto. One night a fairy-godmother sprinkled pixie dust on him and brought him to life. At that moment the strings came off his body. He could now think for himself, speak for himself and even move by himself. He was alive! This excited Geppetto. He celebrated the life of his creation. He did not need to keep Pinocchio on strings, under his restraint and control. Pinocchio was alive and free.

Freedom doesn't excite everybody. There are those who are attracted to Pinocchios on a string. Their satisfaction comes through their ability to successfully and skillfully manipulate another.

As you walk in greater freedom, there will be those who celebrate you and there will be others who use fear tactics in order to keep you in bondage.

There is a counterfeit freedom that comes with the strings. You don't have to manage life's affairs. You don't have to make choices for yourself. You do as you are told. In doing so a certain amount of responsibility is avoided. Sometimes, the strings make us feel safe.

In Exodus 16:3, there is an interesting development. The Israelites begin contemplating the days when they were attached to strings. Rather than remembering the torturous conditions, barbaric job descriptions, and how cruel the Egyptians were to their families, they looked back at their past as if it were the good ol' days. They actually wanted to go back into slavery.

With freedom comes responsibility. When you haven't had to be responsible, there can be an adjustment period after breaking the pattern of control and manipulation. When you cut the strings, you'll be empowered to think for yourself, speak for yourself and move for yourself but if you're not careful in evaluating what pulled you into Egypt in the first place, then it will be just a matter of time before another Egypt lures you into her city limits.

SELF-CONTROL

In a nutshell, our sin has turned us into paranoid androids. We messed up, and now the past has left us feeling exposed and vulnerable. While under the influence of fear and shame, we did the only thing we knew how to do: we attempted to take control, and we've been grasping for control ever since. Biblically, the only person we have permission to control is ourselves. In fact, self-control is a fruit of the spirit. If you are controlling person by nature, perhaps now you may have a better perspective of the motivational factors behind your behavior.

When we sin against God, a series of events are set into motion. The dominos of shame began to fall within our soul and the enemy began to exploit us into self-righteous, fear-based patterns that result in an attempt to control people and even God Himself.

Controlling people control people because their past isn't in their past. It is actually in their future, a hundred yards ahead of them, screaming, "I'm coming to get you and there's nothing you can do about it."

When negative aspects of your past are ever before you, you are forced to do whatever it takes to make sure they don't repeat themselves in the present.

The soul, awakened by shame, kicks into gear declaring, "Don't worry I'll protect you," and just like that the walls go up, the lies begin, and life becomes an evolving snowball of chaos and anarchy. The patterns are copied and pasted over and over again. The desktop of your heart becomes cluttered with situations that will need to be controlled, and within a matter of time you will find that you have become either the puppet or the hand holding the strings. There's no freedom either way.

GOT LOVE?

Despite the fact that I was on my boat fishing on a perfect and sunny Sunday, I was actually quite discouraged. I had just preached a horrible sermon and the devil was beating me up. All these condemning thoughts were coming at me and I really felt like a failure. I needed affirmation. I needed my Father. I began telling the Lord how badly I needed to hear from Him.

"God I know this is immature of me. I know my identity should be rooted in you, but I need to hear from you. I need to know that you are happy with me. I need to know that I'm doing okay. I really need you to speak to me."

This is how I talk to God. My prayer was much longer and far more desperate than described above, but right in the middle of my prayer something violently yanked my fishing rod.

BAM!

The line started ripping out of my reel. I started laughing. It was God. This was His response to me, His fatherly way of saying, "Darren, I'm proud of you."

I fought that fish well. As I pulled it into the boat I started crying, "Thank you Lord, thank you Lord."

There were people outside their homes watching me land the biggest fish that I'd catch that whole season. They must of thought that I was crazy. I was the crying fisherman.

1 John 4:18 says that perfect love casts out all fear. Remove the shame-based fear and you will disempower the motivating factors behind control. In a nutshell, we are incapable of curing ourselves of controlling and manipulative tendencies. What we need isn't behavioral modification. We need love and not just a knowledge of love, but a head-on collision with love. We all need to receive a special token of love from our Father. That undeniable moment when God shows up and puts a huge fish on our line.

I was once at a Chamber of Commerce meeting for our city. A man sitting across the table from me sat back and asked, "Darren, you're a pastor, I have a question for you."

I panicked. I didn't want to do a Q&A in front of everybody. Was he going to ask me about evolution or homosexuality? I started praying.

"Yea, what's up?" I asked confidently.

"Do you believe that someone is born with the capability of loving others or do you believe that a child has to learn to love?"

I started talking and the Holy Spirit hijacked my words.

"I believe that every human has been created by God to love and to give love and that this is our highest call. However, because we are born into a broken world we need to be truly redeemed and restored before we can truly love. This is why attempts to love are so fragmented and distorted from human to human. We desperately crave love but we are unable to find the kind of soul-satisfying love that our hearts long for. I believe we must first find love in God, find restoration in Him before we can begin effectively loving ourselves and others."

"Good answer. I can tell, you have wisdom beyond your years."

That was his give away. He was obviously a believer who had rigged a conversation. He had set me up and in doing so I had presented the gospel to all the business people at that table.

I meant every word I said.

Don't seek God's love as a cure to your control. Receive God's love because His love is receiving you. God's love is not a formula. It's oxygen to your spirit man. Because He loves us, He chooses to not control us. He gives us the freedom to choose Him, to love him and worship Him.

Let us choose to create atmospheres where His love can show up and wreck us. When we know that we are absolutely loved, we don't have to hide and therefore we don't feel any compulsion to take control. When we receive love from God, even when we don't deserve it, we can then extend love quicker to others who don't deserve it.

Perfect love is the perfect pattern interrupt for control. Receive His love each and every day and prepare to have your life absolutely transformed.

3 DIRECTIVES:

- Soak – Soaking is the act of wetting something thoroughly until it's drenched. See yourself as a hard and dry sponge. If you pour a gentle stream of water over the sponge it will simply drip over the sides, but if you plunge the sponge into a bucket of water while squeezing it, it will absorb the water and sink to the bottom of the bucket. Soaking is the act of being plunged into the heart of God and sinking. Soaking is not about praying as much as it is meditating on the Lord and receiving from Him. I recommend soaking music: music that is instrumental, soothing or has simple words that allows you to reflect on God's heart for you. In order to help you out I've created a soaking play list for you at my website: www.isupernaturalist.com/soaking.html. Soaking is a discipline and I'd recommend spending, you guessed it, 20 minutes each day, first thing in the morning, for one week as your primary method of engaging with God.

- Journal - At the end of the day reflect on how your day was different as a result of basking in His presence. Did you feel more focused? Were you less irritable? Did you feel a sense of calm and self-control? Keep track of your progress in your journal.

- Apologize – An apology is the perfect pattern interrupt. When you start to get controlling, apologize. An apology is your sneeze. Seek forgiveness from those you have attempted to control and get ready for a wave of the Holy Spirit to crash over you as He blesses your humility and courage.

SMALL GROUP DISCUSSION QUESTIONS:

- When wrestling with fear how do you manifest control?

- When hurt by someone else how do you manifest control?

- Take a second to ask the Lord to give you a scripture verse for someone in the group. Share the Scripture verses and minister to each other.

ACTIVATION PRAYER:

Father, I come before you with thanksgiving in my heart. Thank you for your love for me. Thank you that I am always welcome to come before you boldly. Your Word says that you are a just judge and so I approach you as my judge and Father. I repent for the sin of control, taking control, controlling others, and manipulation. I repent for using my speech and creative breath, for yelling, swearing, name calling, and being sarcastic or funny in order to keep people away and get my own way. I repent for participating in emotional control, crying, pouting, and using the silent treatment in order to obtain a favorable outcome. I repent for economic control and any way that I have used money to control others. Father, I repent for sexual control and any way that I have been manipulative sexually in order to achieve an outcome or acquire selfish gratification. I repent for physical control and using my size to intimidate other. I repent for violent threats and even violent behaviors as an attempt to get my own way. I repent of any abusive behavior that I have partnered with intentionally or unintentionally. You are not abusive and in abusing others I misrepresented who You are. I repent for partnering with (intentionally or unintentionally) the spirit of intimidation and manipulation. I will partner with them no longer.

Thank you, Father, that I am covered with the blood of Jesus. I am forgiven. 1 John 1:9 says "If we confess our sins, He is faithful and just to forgive us our sins and to cleanse us from all unrighteousness."

Now I ask that you would judge the spirit of control, manipulation, and rebellion on my behalf. In Jesus name, Amen.

WORKSHEET:

- Identify the lie: _____

- Identify the truth that displaces the lie: _____

- Scripture verses to support the truth: _____

RESOURCES FOR THOSE IN ABUSIVE RELATIONSHIPS:

http://www.thehotline.org/

Safety Alert:

Computer use can be monitored and is impossible to completely clear. If you are afraid your internet usage might be monitored, call the National Domestic Violence Hotline at 1–800–799–7233 or TTY 1–800–787–3224.

3
WHO TOLD YOU THAT?

Discerning the Difference Between Facts and Truth

"'I heard the sound of you in the garden, and I was afraid,
because I was naked, and I hid myself." God answered Adam and
asked, "Who told you that you were naked? ..."

– Genesis 3:10-11

WHO TOLD YOU THAT?

My whole life I've believed I was bad at sports. God genetically blessed me with a gift in the arts but deprived me of all hand-and-eye coordination. It wasn't until I was thirty-two years old when the Lord came walking into my garden and asked me why I hid behind humor when playing sports. When I replied that I was bad at sports, He asked me a startling question, "Who told you that?"

LADY GAGA LIED

I read a great book recently called *Talent is Overrated*. And essentially the premise of the book is just that, that talent is overrated. Research is now telling us that great genes don't determine one's greatness. In fact, raw talent has a way of enabling mediocre, or "just good enough" performance. In his book, Geoff Colvin states, "The factor that seems to explain the most about great performance is something the researchers call deliberate practice." This was a revelation! My batting average wasn't determined by my DNA, but rather by my discipline.

May 23, 2011, American singer, Lady Gaga, released her album *Born This Way*. Lady Gaga lied. She wasn't born that way. She confessed in an interview with Neil Strauss several years prior that her childhood was quite pleasant. Lady Gaga actually purposefully subjected herself to a certain level of trauma as an adult because she believed that broken people make for better artists. No, despite what her lyrics say, Gaga wasn't born a superstar. She worked really hard, she sacrificed, and it cost her a lot.

If we're honest, we can't blame our successes or our failures on our DNA. Genetics can be an excuse, or an attempt to justify our hiding.

THE ROOT

I guess I wasn't paying attention. As I looked up at my dad, right there in front of me, flying at my face, was a baseball; it was coming at me in slow motion. The appropriate thing to do would have been to catch it, but, just like that, it picked me up and threw me on my back with a "thud." Birdies began singing, as everything started spinning. I hugged the ground and breathed deeply as I struggled to stay conscious.

That wasn't the only time that happened. A couple years later, my top lip would swell to the point of touching my nose, after being pelted in the face with a soft ball. I chose not to catch that one either.

Physical pain, coupled with embarrassment, left a wound deeper than I had realized. Being a kid, you do what kids do, you shrug things off and you move on. But I didn't like being hurt, and even more, I hated being embarrassed.

Subconsciously I equated sports with physical and emotional pain, and so rather than leaning into the discipline required to be good, I believed a lie: I was bad at sports. If sports = pain, and I didn't like pain, then I'd just make a choice to not like sports.

Humor became my survival mechanism that I used in order to gain acceptance from my peers while attempting to play sports. I'd be funny, and if people laughed, that meant I was accepted. I became a clown on the basketball court, baseball field, volleyball pit, speed skating rink, bob sledding course, and power walking races. My junior year of High School my P.E. teacher asked me if I was mentally challenged. He then proceeded to encourage me to have a conversation with my parents and my doctor regarding my mental wellbeing. I believe all I was doing at that time was jogging around the gym. Apparently my jogging style lacked finesse.

There were two lies that I had believed: first, that I was bad at sports. Second, if I played sports I was going to get hurt. These lies influenced my behavior and impacted my childhood.

GOLDFISH DON'T HAVE SHORT MEMORIES

It's true. We were lied to so we wouldn't feel guilty about putting them in little goldfish bowls. Goldfish are actually smarter than you think; in fact, they are trainable.

You should also know that swallowed gum doesn't remain in your gastrointestinal tract for six months, and cracking your knuckles will not give you arthritis. Who makes this stuff up? I have my theories, but you will have to wait for my next book.

So who told Adam that he was naked?

God questioned Adam's source because He knew that Adam had believed a lie. Adam never did answer God's question.

Most people have no idea that they've been lied to about their identity, nor do they know who actually lied to them. Many people grow up thinking that they are inferior to others, genetically flawed, and less spiritual than others, but who do you think is behind all these lies?

In John 8:44, Jesus refers to Satan as the Father of Lies. This means that in the same way I am responsible for my children's existence, Satan is actually the source and the one responsible for the existence of deception and corruption. He's a thief that comes to steal, kill and destroy. He's a master manipulator and he's committed to doing whatever it takes to keep you stuck in a generational pattern loop. The secret to breaking free is answering God's question, "Who told you that?"

You are not disorganized. You are not a pervert, and no, your hair and nails don't continue to grow after you die. Your goldfish isn't stupid. He's probably brilliant, and there might even be an escape plan in the works that involves catapulting into your toilet while you are sleeping. Help him out and flush him to freedom.

RESTORING THE FOUNDATIONS

"This is a good idea before you get married," is what I was told. It was more than a suggestion; it was a requirement given to me from several leaders who loved me. They all wanted me to go through Restoring the Foundations Ministry, a ministry that deals with four areas: generational sins and curses, ungodly beliefs, life's hurts, and demonic oppression.

I agreed, as I eagerly wanted to get married.

"Darren, how many ungodly beliefs do you think you have?"

I answered, "Around eight."

"You actually have twenty-three."

Several years later, I went through more ministry, a tune up, and we identified several new lies that I had come to believe, including this one:

It's only a matter of time before God's grace lifts and I am left alone to deal with the mess that life creates.

This particular lie would manifest a particular fear-based expectation every Sunday morning. When I'd drive into the church's parking lot, I would have this thought, "I wonder if anyone is going to show up today? Maybe this is the Sunday that no one shows up. Oh well, it was good while it lasted."

The problem with ungodly beliefs is that they create ungodly expectations. The enemy doesn't just want for you to *not* believe, he wants you *to* believe, to expect, to anticipate and to frame up negative events over your life. He wants you to use your creative breath to empower his lies. If the Lord has called us to be the light of the world, you can imagine how excited Satan must get when he can trick believers into manifesting darkness by speaking lies over themselves and others. Paul encourages the saints in 2 Corinthians 10:5 to take every dark and Christ-hostile thought and place it under arrest, handcuff it, put it in prison and throw away the key.

When you find an area of fear within your heart, that pops its mole-like head up from time to time, I would encourage to seek out some intentional ministry. The Lord uses ministers and ministries to help us find our blind spots. You probably don't need deliverance from demons as much as you may need a mind-renewal coach.

*See the resources section at the end of this chapter for my recommendations on trusted ministries with proven track records.

REPROGRAMMING

It's not enough to just stop running the program. A pattern interrupt consists of deleting the program and installing a new program. The goal is to identify the lies and then obtain the appropriate truth that will adequately replace it. This sounds like a daunting process but it's actually quite fun. Identifying lies feels so good, especially when they've been running in the background without our knowledge. A PC needs an antivirus program and we need the Holy Spirit in order to keep a clean operating system. John 16:13 says that the Holy Spirit will lead us into all truth. This means that when a lie is spotted and deleted we simply turn to the Holy Spirit to obtain its replacement.

For example:

Lie: *It's only a matter of time before God's grace lifts and I am left alone to deal with the mess that life creates.*

After praying for about two minutes this is what I heard:

Truth: *God will continue to be faithful to provide everything I need in order to fulfill my desires and His calling on my life.*

The truth brought immediate relief. However, unlike a new operating system on a computer, our minds require adequate time and a prolonged commitment to properly introduce and maintain the newly installed truth. I began proclaiming this truth over my life daily. This is absolutely essential in that truth must be cultivated and assimilated into our souls until it becomes as though we've always believed it. I keep a page on my Evernote app (on my cell phone) titled, "Godly beliefs." This is my truth journal that I can periodically visit from time to time to keep myself sharp and fear-free.

Truth was my pattern interrupt.

The following Sunday I forgot to think about the lie, therefore I forgot to believe it. I parked my car and engaged with my day and when it was all said and done I had this interesting thought, "Wow, I didn't think that thought today."

DEFEATER BELIEFS AND ZOMBIE GOLIATHS

Defeater beliefs are lies that attempt to keep us from operating at our optimum capacity. Defeaters try to keep us from being successful by convincing us that failure is inevitable. Defeater beliefs are Goliaths: giant, intimidating "facts" that attempt to define us and set our boundaries and capabilities. These Goliaths can be overcome with weaponized stones of truth.

Overcoming a defeater belief involves simply identifying the lie, displacing the lie with truth, and then reprogramming the mind with the truth of God's Word. When we fail to retrain the brain, we can experience the resurrection of zombie Goliaths: dead lies that reanimate in order to re-establish dead fortresses of thought.

Just recently a Zombie-Goliath-defeater resurfaced within my mind. I identified it, "Hey, I know you," and I reminded it that it was dead and had no power or authority to creep back into my subconscious. It had no power over me because I didn't tolerate it. I loosed the truth against the lie and it could not remain.

GET GIRDED

A hypothesis for truth is not enough to overcome the enemy. We have to know the truth. That is, we must step into the realm of truth where its realities can be interacted with. "To know," means that we have tasted and seen. We've gone beyond theory and testing and we have literally "girded our loins" with truth.

Ephesians 6:14 says, "Stand firm then, with the belt of truth buckled around your waist…"

This means that truth needs to be put on, like a belt, and worn around our waist. The historical Roman-soldier-belt imagery here is similar to that of a weight belt. It was big and tight, and it would cover the core, from your abs down to the groin-region. Paul is saying, put on your belt of truth because it will strengthen the core of you. We all need core support. We all need the belt of truth.

When we disqualify ourselves from engaging with our dreams because of fear and insecurity, it's important that we take note of the behavior and aggressively pursue truth.

I LOOK UGLY IN THIS PICTURE

I once found myself walking off the stage of an incredible church. It was an honor to speak there and I felt like everything went fairly well. The pastor walked up to me and thanked me for speaking and instead of simply thanking him for the opportunity, I instead responded by tearing myself down, offering a real-time critique of all the areas that I had screwed up. The pastor immediately began to build me up, and even though it felt good, the Lord immediately opened my eyes to the alarming spirit of manipulation that I had engaged with in order to feed my insecurity.

I apologized, "Sorry bro, that was my insecurity speaking." I had caught something in myself that I would need to process with the Holy Spirit.

Since the Lord showed me this behavior, I began to see it in the world around me. People would get on Facebook and post a picture with the comment, "I look so ugly in this picture," and then fifty-plus flattery-based affirmations would follow, praising that person for their undeniable beauty.

We embarrass ourselves when we don't wear our belt. When we know who we are in Christ, we don't have to seek therapy by manipulating our friends. The belt of truth strengthens us to the core of our identity so that we can stand in the kind of strength that is grounded in Christ.

Insecurity is simply the lack of emotional security/support. It's the result of wearing no truth belt. Bill Johnson says it like this, "Insecurity is wrong security exposed," and Bill is right. Insecurity is just an opportunity to learn who we really are in Christ. When we discover truth, we must tighten it around our loins, because it will integrally contribute to the overcoming of life-defining lies.

HOW TO BECOME BARISTA OF THE MONTH

Smile; get positive customer feedback on anonymous surveys; show up to work on time; be liked by your co-workers; execute your duties with excellence; remain mindful of the ideal customer experience and you will become *Barista of the Month*. Your diligence to comply will be rewarded with a Polaroid mug shot of yours truly, scotch-taped to the side of an espresso machine.

Since childhood, we were taught to play it safe, color within the lines, obey the rules and perform for acceptance, but when we grew up we discovered that greatness seemed to be defined by those who, quite frankly, didn't care what anybody thought about them (*i.e. see Jesus*).

How have lies that you've believed caused you to play it safe? When was the last time to you took a risk? When was the last time you got in trouble for something? When was the last time you failed?

Life has a way of becoming a series of predictable pattern loops. Now is your time to disable your autopilot and break the espresso machine.

OVERCOME ORDINARY

"Want to make a billion dollars?" asked Dr. Peter Diamandis - an engineer, physician, and chairman of the X Prize Foundation, "Solve a problem for a billion people."

Whoever told you that being ordinary was the win, lied. Ordinary is overrated. Dr. Diamandis believes that entrepreneurs become billionaires when they are able to solve problems and market the solutions to the issues that ordinary people are complaining about.

And then there is you and me. On the cross, Jesus overcame our ordinariness. He made it possible for us to engage with His extraordinary Kingdom realm simply by faith.

1 Peter 2:9 says, "But you are a chosen race, a royal priesthood, a holy nation, a people for his own possession, that you may proclaim the excellencies of him who called you out of darkness into his marvelous light."

The enemy comes to define our boundaries and capabilities, but as we assimilate our identity into Christ we discover that our "normal" is anything but natural.

Our new nature in Christ redefines who we are, all the way down to our DNA and marrow.

We are supernatural beings, filled with the supernatural purposes of Heaven. We are of a royal priesthood.

We are no longer of this world - mere earth beings - we are now a chosen race; a holy and heavenly nation.

We are possessions of the LORD Himself.

Overcoming ordinary involves seeing yourself for who you are in Him.

The world says, "Close your eyes and visualize the better and perfect *future* version of you," but the Bible says, "You are, NOW, a radical new and Heavenly species."

We are not called to be victims of sovereignty, stuck dab in the bull's-eye of lies, injustice, and stress. We are called to change weather patterns, metaphorically and literally. You are an overcomer, and so I challenge you to overcome the identity that others have tried to cast you in. You are not created in the image and likeness of your tribe. You've been created in the image of God, there is nothing ordinary about HIM, and there's nothing ordinary about you.

3 DIRECTIVES:

1. Identify the lies that you have believed about yourself.

   - "I'm not good at math."

   - "I'm not that spiritual."

   - "I don't hear from God."

2. Record the lies in a journal or note taking app.

3. Ask the Lord what the truth is and displace the lie.

   - Find scriptures that support this truth

   - Renew your mind by declaring these scriptures over your life

SMALL GROUP DISCUSSION QUESTIONS:

- How have lies that you've believed created behavioral patterns?

- How has this process of identifying and replacing lies empowered you?

- How could this chapter influence the way that you see and speak to others?

ACTIVATION PRAYER:

I repent for believing the lie that _____ .

I have believed this to be true and it has contributed to these negative behaviors _____ .

Thank you Father that I am forgiven. Thank you that your blood has cleansed me. I am a new creation.

I dismiss and displace the lie, and I declare the truth that _____

_____ .

I declare…

Scripture 1_____

Scripture 2: _____

Scripture 3_____

*Additional Resources:

Ministries with a proven track record to help you get free, healed, and your mind renewed.

Restoring the Foundations

http://www.restoringthefoundations.org/

West Coast Directors: Walter & Ida Cowart

E-mail: armorbearers@comcast.net

Sozo

http://bethelsozo.com/

Sozo Ministry is available at Seattle Revival Center

office@seattlerevivalcenter.com

424.228.0810

Aslan Place

Personal Prayer Ministry Link:

http://aslansplace.com/language/en/prayer-ministry/

4
THE WINEPRESS IS FOR
WINEMAKING

Dismantling Defeat

*"And without faith it is impossible to please him, for whoever
would draw near to God must believe that he exists and that he
rewards those who seek him."*

– Hebrews 11:6

REVELATORY PERSPECTIVE

Angel of the Lord: Gideon, the Lord is with you!

Gideon: Yea, I doubt that.

Gideon looked like a Seahawk fan following 2015 Super Bowl. The guy
was seriously bummed out. In fact, it was so bad that the angel found
Gideon beating his wheat in a winepress, which is just straight up silly.
Everybody knows that when you thresh wheat, you go up to a high
place where there's good ventilation, but Gideon was down in a grape-
crushing hole, hiding from the Midianites. In the lowest point of
Gideon's life, God came and disrupted his negative mindset with a
prophetic pattern interrupt.

Gideon felt abandoned by God. He felt weak, alone and scared, and
while he was hiding the Lord comes to him and says, "I know who you

are. You are a mighty man of valor, and I'm going to use your might to liberate my people."

Here's the question. Was God lying? Gideon was no warrior, no mighty man of valor, and definitely no liberator. He was a bummed-out coward. Was God flattering him? Trying to say some kind words in order to build up his self-esteem?

If this was a modern story, many people would accuse the Lord of not being very discerning. Gideon had some major issues and God didn't even confront him. It's almost like God wasn't even concerned about his lack of character and faith.

Gideon states the obvious by informing the Lord that his tribe isn't capable of victory. His tribe is literally the weakest tribe in Manasseh. Herein lies a clue as to why the Lord chose Gideon. 1 Corinthians 1:27 says, "But God chose what is foolish in the world to shame the wise; God chose what is weak in the world to shame the strong." Is this not a picture of the gospel? A virgin gives birth to the Messiah in a stable. He would have a carpenter for a father, He would build his tribe with fishermen and tax collectors. He would die on the cross only to be buried in a borrowed tomb.

It's the Superman story; nobody would ever suspect that the nerdy and uncoordinated Clark Kent is actually the city's hero and nobody ever suspected that Gideon would be Israel's next judge.

So the Lord doesn't see a coward, He sees a warrior. But the warrior doesn't see a warrior, he only sees a coward. Instead of stating the obvious, or as many would say "the truth," God speaks to Gideon's identity outside of time. In the present, Gideon is a coward. In the future, he's a hero. God essentially says, I know who you will be so I will declare that future status over your present state.

The revelatory perspective of the Lord created faith within Gideon. God gave Gideon a promise. The promise was His presence.

STATING THE OBVIOUS

Prophecy is the revealing of God's heart. When God's heart is revealed, heavenly perspective is released. It's absolutely critical that a new and healthy prophetic movement begins to emerge on the Earth. Proverbs 19:18 says that without it people will continue to perish.

When the Lord came to Gideon, God's people were suffering because there was no revelatory insight, no heavenly perspective and therefore no plan or strategy to overthrow the grip of the enemy. Because God's heart wasn't being revealed, fear was allowed to permeate the culture.

This is one of many differences between psychics and prophets. Psychics don't know God's heart. They may see up and down a timeline, but all they can do is state the obvious. Prophets have the ability to reveal the hidden things from God's heart, and in so doing they have the ability to release the words needed in order for the enemies of God to be displaced. Just because someone has the ability to state the obvious doesn't mean they're of God, or partnering with His Kingdom mission.

I believe a new prophetic move is being birthed. It's a move that displaces fear by framing true identity. We have to know who we are so we can know what we're capable of. Without heavenly perspective we cannot overthrow the strong grip of the Midianites.

FEAR NOT

In 1 Kings 18, the prophet Elijah engages in one of the coolest revival services of all time, a standoff against the prophets of Baal and Asheer. God shows up, things get crazy, and the false prophets are all slaughtered.

In 1 Kings 19, Jezebel declares her intent to kill Elijah and he takes off running in tremendous fear.

Welcome to the life of a supernaturalist. One day, you raise the dead, and the next, you're wondering if you are even saved. There are too many warriors in wine presses threshing wheat. There are too many dreamers who are afraid to get out of bed and see their dreams become a reality.

THE BATMAN/BOND PRINCIPLE

Elijah was terrified, and so he ran for his life. This behavior is not uncommon of heroes. What do you do when you are being chased down, when the enemy is gaining on you, when you are about to be closed in on? You do what Batman and James Bond do: you instigate a new and unplanned behavior. You apply a pattern interrupt. You do something different. You turn off cruise-control, you stop, and not just stop, you stop abruptly by hitting your e-brake.

The Batman/Bond Principle is simply a strategic U-turn. You'll see it in every action movie. The enemy never sees it coming. You violently change directions and you head right for the enemy. The offensive goes on the defensive, the hawk becomes the chicken, and right as you strategically swerve, the enemy crashes into a gas tanker and blows up.

It's time to pull the e-brake. It's time for a U-turn.

In Judges 6:7, the people of God pull their e-brake. They are done running. They cry out to God and immediately the Lord responds. They had been running from God but now they were running to God. Their self-absorption had cost them their courage and now in their desperation they decided to turn off their autopilot and do something drastic.

People are far too passive when it comes to life change. We say something like, "I need to shave a little body fat." The only thing they end up shaving is some form of body hair. Luke-warmness isn't an option for a champion and so their choices are extreme because they want extreme results. There is no "shaving off a little fat" for a champion. There's just a full on, non-compromising war against fat.

If your enemy is gaining on you, don't keep doing what you're doing. Slam your e-brake, and sling back into the arms of your Father.

DISMANTLING DEFEAT

The original meaning of the word *dismantle* was to remove a cloak. It would later be used as a word to describe the destroying of a defensive capability of a fortification. After the nation busted a U-turn and cried out to God, the Lord came to Gideon and told him that He was going to be the response to their cry. The cloak of defeat was going to be removed from them *and* the enemy was going to have their defensive capabilities removed making them vulnerable.

With the commissioning of the Lord came a supernatural boldness. Gideon was no longer afraid. In Judges 6:28-35, Gideon destroys the altar of Baal and is even given a new name, Jerubbaal, which means *Baal's Contender.* Gideon's mantle of defeat had been removed!

In Judges 6:34, the Lord goes to Gideon and mantles him with Himself, "But the Spirit of the LORD clothed Gideon." The Lord came and put Gideon on like a glove. Paul would experience the same thing, "For me to live is Christ." He's basically saying, "I have become a garment for the Lord to wear on the Earth."

3 PATTERN INTERRUPTS FOR NEGATIVITY

1. Export Praise

    Psalm 148 is one of many praise Psalms that invites everybody, everywhere to engage with creation in nation-changing proclamations that reveal the majesty of God. Praise has a way of recalibrating everything. Praise realigns priorities, values, and practices. When we lose focus of what really matters, it's because we have disengaged with the first commandment - to worship the Lord our God and have no other idols. Praise is a pattern interrupt.

One way to see your praise-life invade your thought-life is to export praise from your heart onto paper. This is what David did, because, let's face it our minds can be a hectic place. Multiple studies show that people process on a deeper level when they write things down; it has a way of solidifying truth within our subconscious.

Begin a praise journal. Begin by writing down the things you are thankful for. Ascribe value to the Lord. Reflect on His faithfulness and find a creative way to articulate your thankfulness. Engage in this activity each morning. Perhaps one morning you may only write a sentence. Don't worry, there will be other mornings where rivers of praise pour out onto your pages.

2. Be Childlike

There was this time in my life when the winds of change began blowing violently and, quite frankly, it was frightening. I felt like I was surfing a gigantic wave but my posture was off. Whereas most surfers stand on a surfboard, I was laying on my belly, holding on for dear life, screaming like a girl. On one hand it was exciting, on the other hand I felt like I was going to die. I asked a good friend of mine for prayer and it was almost as if he was laughing at me. He responded via text message, "Just remain childlike and everything will be fine." It was some of the best advice I'd ever received.

Childlikeness is a pattern interrupt. When I feel like my beliefs are being challenged, when I feel overwhelmed, when I become fearful, when my analyzing becomes paralyzing, I remember the text message, "Darren, be childlike."

3. Practice Teamwork

Even though it takes a team to win a game, our Western culture has an obsession with superstars. We are a celebrity-driven culture that puts the best player on the cover of Sports Illustrated instead of celebrating the true players and factors that contributed to their success.

Every society has idols, and in America it tends to be the person looking at us in the mirror. The problem with individualism is that it creates a narcissistic culture of isolation where we don't function as a body, but rather as a bunch of random body parts, scattered about, trying to be the full meal deal.

Teamwork is a great pattern interrupt for negativity. We all need to be reminded that God never called us to be the King of the Sandbox. We've been invited to be a part of the Ecclesia: a governmental garment that's been knit by the Lord to function within the heavens and the earth. Christianity is inescapably corporate. We're in this together, and so we might as well take responsibility for the lack of unity within the Bride of Christ and start intentionally creating opportunities for Kingdom collaboration wherever we have influence.

A NEW VIEW

Sometimes when facing discouragement and negativity we just need a change of scenery or a new view. In Genesis 15, Abraham was seriously bummed out. He and his wife Sara had no son, no heir, and now they were looking at writing one of their servants into their will to be an inheritor. God comes and visits Abraham, but all he can do is groan and complain about being childless. Abraham needs a serious pattern interrupt.

The Lord is basically like, "Dude, you need some fresh air. Let's step outside this tent for a second."

Abraham steps outside and the Lord commands him to look up.

"You see those stars, Abraham? I'd like for you to count them."

Abraham takes in the new view, the crisp night air, and the layers upon layers of stars that fill the heavens. Abraham is overwhelmed by the request that he almost forgets to breathe.

"God, I can't count them. They are innumerable."

"Exactly." God responds, "I'm about to overwhelm you with blessing. Abraham you have asked me for a son - one star - but I'm about to make a nation out of you, and from this nation will come my only begotten son who will save humanity from her sins."

God had to take Abraham outside of his tent because there was nothing inside the tent that would communicate the scale of favor God had in mind. Abraham's dream could have been fulfilled within his tent. His tent was plenty big enough for a new addition to the family, but God's dream would have never fit inside that tent. God had to take him outside of his world and invite him into the limitless expanse of the heavens so he could see the dream of God.

Too many times we dream inside our homes, businesses, regions, and church buildings. We dream and then we get frustrated. The Lord wants to take us outside. He wants for us to not only look up, but go up, and begin dreaming within the context of the nations and the heavens.

BELIEVE GOD

After God reveals His plan to Abraham, Genesis 15:6 says, "And he believed the LORD, and he counted it to him as righteousness."

This is where it gets real. At the end of the day, the movie or the book, you have to ask yourself the question, "So what?" After the Lord speaks to you, will your life just go on as usual? Will you pretend as though nothing has happened? Will you just wait and see if God is a man of His word?

The word of the Lord always deserves a response. Abraham's response was exactly what the Lord was looking for. He believed.

There's about to be a resurgence within the faith movement. The voices of faith such as Kenyon, Copeland, and Hagin are about to make a comeback, and there will also be others, new voices, and fresh revelation concerning belief. There's a fresh gift of faith being released on the earth at this time that we need if we wish to participate with the dreams of God in our generation. There's about to be a generation on the earth whose faith is pleasing to the Lord. Like Abraham, we will respond with unwavering belief in the Lord.

My generation has been plagued with chronic depression, PTSD, ADD, ADHD, and bipolar, amongst numerous other psychological conditions. The pattern interrupt for these ailments is faith. It's a substance. It's a key. It's the gateway by which the dreams of God are manifested through His sons and daughters.

Within the context of His presence, childlikeness, and community, we can contend for a full manifestation of His Kingdom on the earth. We don't have to be beat up by the spirit of fear and unbelief. We can actually intimidate the enemy with the substance of things hoped for and about to be seen.

THE WINEPRESS IS FOR WINEMAKING

No more threshing wheat in the winepress, hiding in a place of fear and unbelief while entertaining frustration in your heart. The winepress is for winemaking. Biblically, wine is symbolic of joy and covenant relationship. It's time to shift from a season of surviving into a season of overcoming.

You aren't a coward. You're a mighty man of valor. The Lord is calling you to come into the fullness of your identity in Him. He's removing the mantle of defeat and clothing you with Himself.

Leave your comfort zone, your shanty, your ghetto. It's time to get outside. It's time to explore the night sky. There are things he hasn't shared with you yet. He's just waiting for the right time and place.

Create that moment. Set a date to discuss His dreams for your life, and when He reveals to you the dreams and desires of His heart, don't get negative. Engage your faith, and regardless of how you feel, declare your confidence in your King.

3 DIRECTIVES:

1. Identify and disempower disappointment within your heart.

   - Where do you feel that the Lord has let you down? Be specific.

   - Repent for allowing disappointment to keep you in a place of striving and fear.

2. Count the stars: Dream bigger dreams by seeing God's desires for your life.

   - Set bigger goals.

3. Pick a team.

   - Are you in isolation? Are you plugged into a local church? Do you prefer to be alone? Break alliance with the spirit of Michael Jordan and join a team.

SMALL GROUP DISCUSSION QUESTIONS:

- Can you identify with Gideon or Abraham?

- What is the Lord saying to you now?

- How has it been difficult to believe God?

ACTIVATION PRAYER:

Father, I declare my intention to listen and be obedient to your voice. I declare that I am where You have called me. You have positioned me here and now, in the center of your will. You have placed me underneath the waterfall of Your blessings. Let them pour down upon me and spread out beyond me because of my response to Your voice.

May the Lord be glorified in my city because of me.

May the Lord be glorified in my country because of me.

May the Lord be glorified through my children's prosperity because of me.

May the Lord be glorified through my finances and investments.

May the Lord be glorified through my work and worship.

I declare that the Lord is my refuge and that I am safe and secure in Him.

I declare that I have been called to be blessed.

The best days of my life are yet to come.

I declare that I have been called to live my life under the banner of the Name of my God. His righteousness is at work in me. I am a part of a Holy priesthood. I am a child of promise and inheritance.

My friends, family and neighbors will be able to clearly see the favor of the Lord that has rested upon me and they will stand in awe of God's grace that has settled down upon me and my family.

The blessing of Heaven that is upon me is generational. The Lord has promised to lavish good things upon me, that flow down upon my children, their children, and their children's children.

I declare that the heavens have been opened above me, His sky vaults have been opened, and that everything I need is easily accessible in and through my Father of Lights.

I will use my resources and abundance to bless others. I will graciously and generously help those who cannot afford it or deserve it. By God's grace I have been blessed and now by God's grace I will bless others.

I am a King and a priest. I have been given authority in the heavens and the Earth. The voice of the Lord is my guide, for He is my Shepherd.

I will not compromise my values, ethics, or beliefs. I will hold fast to the Word of the Lord. I will love the Lord my God and serve Him only.

Amen.

5
TAP DANCING FOR JESUS

Why We Do the Silly Things We Do

"How precious to me are your thoughts, God! How vast is the sum of them! Were I to count them, they would outnumber the grains of sand -when I awake, I am still with you."

- Psalm 139:17-18

WOOKIE WATER

If you ever buy a pet fish, you will be advised to fill the tank with tap water and leave it for a few days before you introduce the fish to his new home. This process is meant to off-gas the chlorine. There's the possibility that the chlorine in your tap water could kill your fish if you put it in too soon. The water that comes out of your faucet has been pumped through miles of piping that consist of varying materials, from plastic, to copper, to lead, in varying states, age, and corruption, before arriving at your faucet. For this reason, bottled water is more expensive than gasoline.

Have you ever bought a bottle of water from the grocery store? It's overwhelming. There's the water that flows from the mystical Canadian glaciers that nourishes unicorns and moose, there's the water that's been gathered from the ancient wells of Fiji that removes chest hair and adds seven days of life for every ounce consumed, and then there's the 99 cent gallon of water that was boiled in a styrofoam factory and is useful for washing dishes when you go camping. Each company claims that their water is the purest. However, most of the big companies use the same water sources that municipal water comes from. Some even buy the municipal water, filter and treat it, and then bottle and sell it. So your $8-dollar bottle of Wookie Water may not actually be from the magical forest of Endor. Most bottled water is just slightly better than tap water, poured into a carcinogenic plastic bottle and slapped with a pretty label. Bottled water is overseen by the FDA instead of the EPA – as with municipal water – and so it is actually less monitored than municipal, especially if it is sold within the state where it was bottled.

Do you know what's in your water, theologically speaking? What do we do when we find out that something we've been drinking isn't necessarily all that healthy? How do we allow for the Lord to interrupt our understanding of ourselves and Him, even if it's contrary to what we have been taught traditionally?

CONFUSED BAPTICOSTAL

When I was twenty-three, I was given a CD of a pastor who was teaching through the book of Genesis. The particular sermon I listened to covered the story of Jacob and Rachel and it rocked my world. As I listened to the sermon, I found myself laughing and repenting; I was hooked. This dude was preaching through the whole book of Genesis, chapter by chapter, verse by verse, and it was absolutely fascinating. He talked about chicks, beer, Jesus, and salvation through grace alone; it was like biting into a delicious T-bone steak for the very first time.

Even though I was raised in the church, I don't remember ever hearing expository preaching. I knew revival church, and religious church, but I didn't know chicks-beer-Jesus-Bible-teaching-church. I was proud of my flag-waving revival church because we were passionate and wild in our worship, but we didn't have what this guy had.

I started downloading every sermon I could find by this guy, and if he mentioned mentors, role models, or friends, I'd listen to their stuff too. Before I knew it I was attending two churches, and even considered membership at two churches. My wife and I actually did our premarital process at this church because their marriage process was so thorough, and we could be involved without anyone knowing who we were (the beauty of a mega church).

I am so thankful to the Lord for this church, and for the pastor. This pastor has influenced me more than any other pastor, and I absolutely respect and honor him, and I'm not going to tell you who it is, although you probably already know.

On one hand, I was learning the Bible, theology, doctrine, and new words like "propitiation". On the other hand I was becoming very judgmental and critical. I found myself getting in debates with good pastors who loved me over such topics such as "Depravity versus Christ's righteousness"; and at one point I even told Pastor Gail that women shouldn't be pastors and that when I became a pastor I would not allow women elders. She was very gracious with me. She should have punched me in the mouth.

Without knowing it, I had swallowed the blue pill; I had become a *Bapticostal,* a reformed Spurgeonite, getting credentials with the Assemblies of God. I was reading a lot of John Piper's stuff. I even heard Piper preach in person a few times and I always had this feeling that Piper really loves God, but if he knew me, he'd hate me, and unlike Gail would definitely try to punch me in the mouth.

Before I started attending the reformed church, I was backslidden. As a screwed up young man, I loved the doctrine of total depravity before I ever knew there was such a doctrine. I could remain a depraved worm and still be saved by grace. I could relate with the dichotomy of being "positionally" righteous and yet practically shady. I would have big arguments with Gail's associate pastor, Greg Daley. His was a big E.W. Kenyon guy who loved the topic of righteousness and Christians being the righteousness of Christ Jesus. We would argue about whether or not we were sketchy sinners saved by grace or whether we were righteous sinless sons who can actually choose to not sin because of grace. I was determined that Greg was nuts.

Anytime I was told that I was awesome, I would say, "No I'm not, but God is awesome." It sounded so humble, but the problem was that I wasn't humble. As long as I could berate myself and talk God up then I didn't have to be accountable to any standard.

Let me be clear, I'm not saying that Calvinists are hypocrites. I was a hypocrite and honestly, at that particular time, I couldn't have even told you who John Calvin was. I sewed together a custom set of doctrines like fig leaves that would let me keep my Christian title while not having to live up to any particular standard. When I started to really study Calvinism I was hungry for boundaries and rules. I wanted some good old-fashioned fundamentalism and even though I have gone a different direction theologically, I don't regret those years of services, conferences and countless hours of downloaded teaching.

COMING OF AGE

My Calvinistic world began to crumble when I hit the realities of pastoral ministry. I was installed as pastor in 2009. I believed that our church was about to explode with such unprecedented growth that I was going to have to beg God to stop sending people. The transition into pastoring was absolutely greased by the grace of God and the loving patience of our leadership and people, and yet I found myself confronted with actual ministry reality. Our church numbers did not immediately increase. In fact, people began dying. I performed back-to-back funerals for a mother with cancer and her daughter who returned back to drugs and died of a skin infection. I officiated another set of back-to-back funerals for a son and his mother who both died of cancer just months apart. One day as I was driving to go pray for a woman in our church fighting for her life. I got angry.

"God! I'm not going to go and pray for this woman just because it's my pastoral duty. Do you still heal people or what? I know that you can, but why don't I believe that you want to do it today? I'm NOT just going to go and pray for this woman that she would be cheered up. I want her to be healed."

I didn't know if I was the problem or He was the problem. That's when I realized that I was having an identity crisis. I was a fragmented pastor; one minute jumping around like a tent meeting revivalist and the next doubting God's willingness to heal.

Do I pray, "Oh Lord, if it be thy will," or do I act like Jesus and say, "Woman, thou art healed!" I didn't even know what I believed and it bothered me.

In that moment the Holy Spirit came into my car and infused me with faith. I walked into her room like Jesus approaching Lazarus's tomb. I was going to kill that cancer. I issued a cease and desist order on the spirit of infirmity. I prayed with boldness and authority. I wasn't afraid. Shortly after, I conducted her funeral. This, however, was not a defeat. God was awakening something in me.

I got my hands on everything I could that dealt with the doctrine of healing. I read Smith Wigglesworth's biography, listened to Bill Johnson's teaching on Healing: The Neglected Birthright. And I watched Randy Clark's Healing School conducted at Bethel Church in Redding.

This is when I learned that I had been drinking too much chlorine. I made a decision: I was going to be a revival pastor. I believed in this stuff.

I began purging my defeater beliefs and studying what the Bible had to say about the gifts of the spirit, the authority of the believer, and the nature and character of a Christian. My transformation was beginning.

It didn't take long before I was learning about my identity in Christ. I became hooked on Romans, Ephesians, and Galatians. My bar was being raised by scripture instead of by man's interpretation of it. I learned that before Christ I was completely depraved, but after Christ I was a new creation. I learned that grace isn't just for the forgiveness of sin, but empowerment to not have to sin. I learned that I wasn't a worm, I wasn't a sinner, I wasn't shady, I wasn't naked and cold trying to buy gold, but that I was a son, a saint, righteous, clothed, and wealthy because of the extravagant and costly blood of Jesus.

I thought that I was an isolated case, but I quickly learned that there were others that were drinking the same water as me. I needed a personal theological pattern interrupt, and then I needed grace for those who hadn't yet arrived at the same conclusion as me.

I appreciate the diversity within the Kingdom of God and yet I must be frequently reminded that the Kingdom is all about the King. Our understanding is limited. We see through a glass darkly, and because of this we must be constantly learning, repenting and growing. When the Holy Spirit reveals to us theological distortions, we must remember that this revelation is for the purpose of falling deeper in greater love with Jesus. With revelation comes responsibility to reveal the character and nature of God in a clearer and more truthful way. We are all coming of age, transitioning into a greater understanding of sonship, and are being entrusted to a greater measure of responsibility.

HOW TO WALK OUT A THEOLOGICAL PATTERN INTERRUPT

1. Shame not.

    Don't treat others as less intelligent; don't refer to people as ignorant or unenlightened. If you start treating people on your team as though they are the enemy, you are most likely being used by the enemy to bring division and discord.

2. Check the fruit.

    If no one sees the fruit of your theological pattern interrupt, if no one is asking you if you've changed your medication, if you don't see a difference in your awe levels for the presence of the Lord, then check the branch your new belief is growing on.

3. Stay humble.

    1 Corinthians 8:1 says that knowledge puffs up, but love builds up. When our foundation shifts from love to knowledge the integrity of our ministry becomes compromised.

WHY PEOPLE HATE LAMBORGHINIS

People who hate Lamborghinis are people who can't afford Lamborghinis; by passing judgment it's easier for us to cope with this reality. We do it all the time. We make blanket statements about rich people, poor people, lawyers, politicians, doctors, dentists, pastors, clowns, whatever. Instead of confronting our insecurities we drop unfounded statements about others because it makes us feel superior.

The truth is that people hate Lamborghinis because of what they stand for. They represent excessiveness, abundance, and more than enough. When a Lamborghini drives by, it can have a way of making us feel poor and insignificant, but the car isn't really the problem; it's just revealing something deeper about our identity and how we see ourselves. When people say that they hate God, or the church, or Christians, they are basically hating on the Lamborghini. They hate God, because they feel shamed by Him.

The thought is, "I could never be good enough to actually deserve God's love. In fact, most likely, God hates me because of all the evil I have done."

When a person like this is confronted with Christian culture it triggers their rejection; it amplifies their shame; it makes them want to lash out because, after all, Lamborghinis are just stupid cars made for pompous and entitled people.

The existence of God forces us to confront our existence. His mercies force us to confront our judgments. His love forces us to confront our bitterness. Sometimes, His perfection is overwhelming, similar to a Lamborghini, and many people feel like they just can't measure up.

Good news. You don't need to hate Lamborghinis, because, you're not poor.

You don't need to hate the couple at church that have been married for a hundred years, because, your divorce does not define you.

You don't need to hate Christians, because, you can also have *Joy, Joy, Joy, Joy, Down in Your Heart* as well.

PATTERN INTERRUPT FOR HATE

1. Don't be shamed by other people's abundance; this kind of judgment will anchor you to lack.

2. Stop coveting; because in doing so you are saying, "God you have not been faithful within my life."

3. Celebrate those who are ahead and beyond you. Celebration requires humility and the Lord exalts the humble.

4. Practice thanksgiving; be mindful of your blessings and give credit where credit is due: the LORD.

TAP DANCING FOR DUMMIES

Tap dancing is unlike any other kind of dance in that blind people can enjoy it. Try it. Close your eyes and YouTube a tap dance performance. You can almost see it with your eyes shut. It's fun, and so dang noisy.

When you tap dance, you become both a musician and a dancer. Tap dancers get the attention on the stage; they are the main attraction.

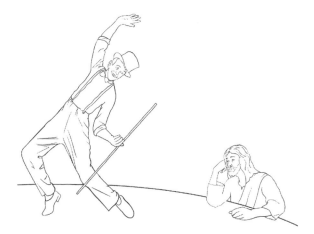

How does a Kia become a Lamborghini? The Kia must learn to tap dance, perform, and earn the attention of the crowd.

Religion is the attempt to be something that you aren't; to earn something that you really don't deserve. Religion says, "You aren't a Lamborghini, so just pretend to be one, and in time, you (and maybe a few others) will believe the act."

How alive is your relationship with Jesus? Is there any walk behind your talk?

Perhaps it's time for a religious pattern interrupt; time to take off the tap dancing shoes and to launch them at the spotlights. After all, the cruelest part of religious performance is that while our own soul craves the praises of man, the enjoyment is limited because of self-condemnation. Many times we seek affirmation from people because we are afraid that we will never measure up to God. The enemy is then able to take that very same performance and shame us, rubbing our (behind-the-curtains) hypocrisy in our face. The cross is God's pattern interrupt for religious performance. The crucifixion of Jesus was the very antithesis of performance. On the cross we see the truest and purest form of love and vulnerability. The cross is our invitation to be fully us.

He, in His perfection, became our faulty religious tap dancing performance so we could be absolutely righteous. You are absolutely loved and accepted because of Jesus. You are qualified for ministry because of Jesus. You can be used by the Lord to do crazy things because of Jesus.

Don't be distracted by the deficiencies of your DNA. Marvel at the perfection of His DNA that has overwritten the insufficiencies of yours. His love redeems and restores. His love creates and perfects. His love is active and alive inside of you. Don't fight His love. Surrender to it. Partner with it. Dance with it.

IT'S NOT FOR THEM, IT'S FOR YOU

How often do you prophesy over yourself? You may wonder if that's even legal. Many people spend thousands of dollars traveling the globe, attending every prophetic conference on this side of the galaxy. They are fishing for a prophetic word, something magical, something that they could have probably landed years ago without leaving their bed.

Steve Backlund, from Bethel Church in Redding, CA, walked us through an activation where he asked all of us to get a prophetic word for someone in the room and write it down. He surprised us by saying that the word wasn't for them, but rather for us. He then explained that most people are incapable of receiving amazing words from the Lord for themselves, but are perfectly capable of getting something from the Lord for someone else. Receiving affirmation from the Lord is crucial in breaking religion's pattern loops. The best way to refresh your theology is to begin receiving understanding from the heart of God, and then find Biblical evidence that can solidify that truth.

You have permission to receive truth from God; directly from God. Jesus replaced the middleman. You don't need a psychic, a medium, or a guide. You don't even need another conference. You just need to know that you have access to your Father's heart because of Jesus.

Get a word from the Lord, for you. Get a bunch of them. Write them down. Revisit them. He's a good father that is so generous with His presence and words of affection.

RECEIVING AS A CORE VALUE

If we are not able to receive praise and thanks for a job well done, then mostly likely our problem isn't our theology; our theology is just the Band-Aid that's covering our shame based thinking. Shame won't allow one to receive credit for anything. If we live our lives shaming ourselves because of our inadequacies, we will absolutely forbid others from recognizing us for our achievements. It gets worse, when we wrestle with shame-based thinking, we may actually sabotage our own success so that we won't have to receive praise.

Sometimes when shamed, there can be a part of our heart that believes we deserved the punishment. Whenever something cruel happens, it's easy to entertain the notion that the negative event is God's punishment for something in our past.

I spent some time recently engaging the Lord by singing portions of the Song of Songs. It was so humbling because typically my worship consists of Psalm-like expressions of gratitude to the Lord. The Song of Songs is almost a response to the Psalms. It's as though we get to hear what the Lord is singing as He dances and rejoices over us.

No Christian can argue that praise and worship should be a regular part of the believer's walk, but we haven't yet learned the importance of receiving praise and affirmation from our Father.

Religion attempts to keep us so busy performing that we never have the time for receiving. Receiving should be a core value for every Christian. We were created to receive; wired by the hands of God with five senses - like an antenna - and what do antennas do? They receive.

HOW TO PRACTICE SABBATH AS A PATTERN INTERRUPT

1. Take a break.

   Sabbath doesn't mean that you quit everything, it just means that you are taking a break from everything. How long has it been since you've taken a break from everything? Sometimes we don't need to quit, sometimes we just need to take a break.

2. Schedule rest.

   For me, if it's not on my schedule, it's probably not going to happen. Did you know that the Hebrews were allowed to be intimate within the context of marriage on Sabbath? It's okay to schedule intimacy, to schedule rest, to schedule dates. We schedule what we value. Make rest a part of your rhythm.

3. Communicate.

   Sometimes we don't communicate our need for rest because we are afraid that it's going to indicate weakness or poor lifestyle choices, but even God rested after He created the world and there's no weakness in him. Be straight up about your need for rest and communicate when you are resting.

4. Don't Feel Guilty

   Only you can take care of yourself. If you really are a temple of the Holy Spirit don't you think you ought to take care of your temple? Sleep; eat well; exercise; make time for you. When you suffer, everybody else suffers. Don't apologize for practicing Sabbath rest.

SEXUAL ADDICTION

Sexual addiction has nothing to do with sex. I have seen a theme established from the proven track of several counselors that say the secret to overcoming sin is not to become more sin conscience. Many counselors don't even address the specifics of their client's sins. The secret to successfully overcoming sexual addiction is to remove the embedded shame. In a nutshell, remove the shame and you'll remove the stronghold.

The pattern interrupt for porn is the presence of God. He wants to be invited into that place of secrecy, shame and isolation.

A friend of mine battled a serious porn problem for years. One day Jesus spoke to him and said, "Bring me with you." So he did! There he was, looking at inappropriate images, asking Jesus what he thought about the women he was looking at, and you know what, Jesus told him what He thought. His freedom wasn't immediate but he eventually got completely set free.

When the Lord started to speak to him about these women a new sense of value was created. All of a sudden they were no longer objects; they were daughters. In this process the Lord started to remap his brain and as his mind was renewed his heart was restored. He repented, confessed his addiction to his wife and began talking about how serious his addiction was. The Lord stepped into the darkness, bringing light, forgiveness, truth and freedom.

If you want to love God with all your heart then you have to invite God to inhabit all your heart, even the yucky places. God isn't intimidated by our chaos. There's no place that He would rather be than in the middle of your darkness.

He's waiting for your invitation.

PORN PATTERN INTERRUPT

1. Share

    Don't let the enemy shame you any longer. Find someone you can trust, who is free in the area that you are struggling and begin the process of honest conversation and dialogue. You will feel 1000 lbs. lifted off your chest once you do.

2. Declare

    The enemy uses our sin to subconsciously define us. As we declare the truth of God's word, those defeater beliefs begin to peel off our minds. Your new identity will bare new fruit. Begin to declare over yourself who you are in Him. For example, "I am righteous," "I am holy," "I am pure," and "I am clean."

    When you're tempted simply remind yourself, "I cannot engage with that because, I am holy, pure and clean."

3. Struggle

    Struggle does not equal sin. You have permission to struggle, but you do not have to sin. You struggle because you are human. Every person struggles with something different; but make a choice to not struggle alone. In isolation, struggles usually turn into sinful situations, but in community struggles can result in victory.

HE LOVES ME SO I LOVE ME

When Jesus said in Matthew 22:39, "Love your brother as you love yourself," He was actually commanding us to step into a healthy place of self-love. This is not permission to be a narcissist (so stop taking selfies in the mirror of your bathroom: #biceps, #abs, #health, #tan, #iworkout).

In order to love yourself biblically you need to fall in love with "the you" that the Lord loves. Often times when people fall in love with themselves they are actually partnering with pride and loving the parts of themselves that they feel are superior to others. This is not what we are talking about. Loving yourself in a biblical and healthy way means that you see yourself the way that the Lord sees you: forgiven, pure, holy, righteous, unashamed and fearfully made.

When we love ourselves in Him, because of Him, we are actually loving ourselves not unto our own glory but unto the glory of the Lord.

It's a revelation, "He loves me, so I love me."

David wasn't full of himself when he proclaimed, "I praise you for I am fearfully and wonderfully made." In Psalm 139:14, David is pondering the complexity and intricacy of his own creation. He is marveling in the reality that he is a manifestation and fulfillment of a God dream. While considering his birth and his humanity his heart isn't filled with pride but rather unexplainable gratitude. Imagine if every time you looked in the mirror you broke out singing spontaneous worship songs. Instead, when many people look in the mirror they break out singing the blues. The mirror is where we usually fall into hardcore self-criticism mode. Our attention is immediately drawn to our hair (or lack thereof), our abs (or lack thereof), or our nose hair (or abundance thereof). Non-

Christians and Christians alike are equally hard on themselves and I would argue that many Christians are actually even harder on themselves than non-Christians because they have just enough of the law in them to leave their conscience in perpetual self-judgment mode.

Psalm 139:17-18 David says, "How precious to me are your thoughts, God! How vast is the sum of them! Were I to count them, they would outnumber the grains of sand -when I awake, I am still with you."

I have heard very few believers talk this way. Can you imagine your pastor getting up this Sunday and saying, "God thinks that I am the most amazing man in the world? He loves the way I talk. He loves my smile. He loves my preaching style. He thinks I'm an amazing father. He thinks I'm an amazing husband..."

But, if your pastor said, "Look, I'm just a screw up like you. I mess up all the time. Thank you God for your grace." That might seem perfectly normal, healthy and maybe even humble.

The Library of Congress couldn't contain all the kind and gracious thoughts that the Lord has regarding you. In fact, every book, in every library, in every nation could not contain all of the loving thoughts that the Lord has regarding you. In light of this, stop trash talking yourself, God thinks you're awesome because you are.

WINDS OF CHANGE

We really have to make a conscious choice not to partner with the spirit of religion, but rather with the spirit of grace, with the spirit of acceptance, and with the spirit of Christ Jesus.

Now is the time. You are being released like a leaping calf from the stall. You have permission to be alive, to be you, and to be with Him. Take off your grave clothes and step into the light that is in Him. Acknowledge and embrace the mystery of union and His promise to be your companion. The night is turning to day, not because of the dawning sun, but rather because of the dawning sons. The family of God is growing and glowing, radiating and emanating the living atmospheres of Heaven. It's time to shine, to be seen, to be heard, and to reveal the one whose breath contains unlimited creative power.

Don't adapt your theology to conform to your inadequacies. Conform your inadequacies to adapt to your theology.

You don't have to tap dance anymore. Take off your tap dancing shoes. You bring God the most glory when you are the most comfortable in your own shoes.

3 DIRECTIVES:

1. Create a stop doing list.

   What things have you done because you've been told you have to? What things are you doing because it's what people have demanded of you? Where have you quit caring but are still serving? Surrender it to the Lord, communicate it to others and set an expiration date. Be humble, flexible and responsible with the date. Finish any commitments that you have made. Don't do anything crazy that's going to involve losing a ton of cash. Be wise and stop tap dancing (doing those things that are not rewarding and very consuming).

2. Start doing list.

    Begin a start doing list. What could you start doing in order to get the romance back into your relationship with the Lord and your spouse? What can you begin doing to let people know that you care about them?

3. Communicate.

    Make a commitment to communicate to those you love and trust the areas where you are overcommitted and under committed. Be accountable for your pattern interrupt. Communicate to others your vision and where you feel the Lord is calling you.

SMALL GROUP DISCUSSION QUESTIONS:

- How have others defined you based on what you do; has that been a positive or negative thing?

- How do you feel pressure to perform; what motivates that pressure?

- How has your theology changed over the years, and how has the Lord used different seasons of understanding to shape you?

ACTIVATION PRAYER

You are my father, my protector and my shepherd. I declare I can trust you because you love me and you want the best for me. I declare that I do not have to pretend or perform in order to look, sound, or appear a certain way. My acceptance is unconditional because of the sacrifice of

Your son. There is nothing I can do to make You love me more, and there's nothing I can do to make you love me less.

You are my resting place. I find my peace within your presence. As I rest in you, you restore the parts of my life that have been fractured because of sin. You are the spirit of revival and you are reviving me. I am coming alive in your presence.

I declare that I don't have to be afraid anymore. I don't care what people think about me because I know what you think about me. I am allowed take risk. Failing a task does not make me a failure. You are my success, my courage, my strength, and my rest.

There is no darkness in you, and I choose to not tolerate darkness within me. Search me, know me, and set me a part unto yourself.

I receive your love. I receive your grace. I receive my new identity that is found in your identity. As you reveal me, let me reveal you. I love who you are and all that you stand for.

As I rest, flex your strength in me, all for Your glory, in Jesus' name, AMEN.

6
THE RUMBLERS

New Breed, Pattern Interrupters

"⁶ For this reason I remind you to fan into flame the gift of God, which is in you through the laying on of my hands, ⁷ for God gave us a spirit not of fear but of power and love and self-control."

- 2 Timothy 1:6-7

I HEAR THE SOUND OF ONE CRYING, AND HE'S STANDING ON A SEVEN-FOOT-TALL WOODEN SEAL

I started with the story of Noah's Ark - which seemed appropriate considering I was standing on seven-foot-tall wooden seal - and then I continued barking out every Bible story I knew. A crowd was gathering to hear me - a seven-year old preacher on a gospel vendetta. I began a new story - yelling at the top of my lungs - a new story of a man who disobeyed God and found himself in the belly of a whale. I would have climbed on top of the sea horse except it was like twenty feet tall, so I made the seal work.

A man recorded me on his VHS camcorder (that was so huge it had to rest on his shoulder). My friends watched in delight and snapped pictures which grace their photo albums to this day.

Preaching was in me like basketball was in Michael Jordan, housekeeping in Martha Stewart, and kicking terrorist's butts in Jack

Bauer. I didn't realize it then, but I was a street preacher, and not like the ones who wear sandwich board signs with the Hell's ten-day forecast, I was different. I was a rumbler in the making.

I preached all the time, and everywhere. My parents have videos of me preaching before I could even speak English. Sometimes I had a microphone and sometimes I had to shout.

One early morning I started preaching real loud, my high pitch squeal sounded awesome as it bounced off the houses in our cul-de-sac and reverberated back at me. This was my packed stadium, although nobody was around to hear me, it wouldn't have bothered me if they could. Knowing that nobody was listening boosted my confidence. I preached like a revivalist, shouting as if it were the last days. All of a sudden a loud amplified voice filled the cul-de-sac via their intercom system.

"Go home, Darren!"

It scared me so bad that I high tailed it home. I found a quiet place to catch my breath and process what had just happened.

How long had they been listening?

Did this mean that my neighborhood wasn't fond of street preaching?

We'd have to move.

I didn't realize it, but the Lord was preparing me then, for now. There was an embryonic rumble in me as a child that desired to disrupt things.

There is a shaking in the present that isn't random. For generations, intercessors have been contending for such a time as this. Heaven is being released onto the earth, bringing about a shaking, via a new breed of pattern interrupters, or what I'll refer to as *the rumblers*.

The rumblers are coming of age. They aren't just screaming in microphones at revival conferences or gathering around round-tables, discussing higher-level apostolic secrets; they teach your children, make your mochas, fix your teeth, and create your kids' video games. They are the ones who are legislating in Congress, and in the Heavens. This is not an add-on to a seven-mountains strategy. This is a Heavenly strategy, and if you're striving to make culture renewal happen, you may be missing out.

THE AUSTRALIAN RUMBLER

We were disappointed to hear that the Senior Pastor wasn't speaking. He seemed cool. He was bald and Scottish, and the lead pastor of a growing Australian church located on Queensland's Gold Coast. I wanted to hear Sean Connery preach, but now we were getting passed off to his youth pastor, who had just washed down his Red Bull with a Rock Star. My wife and I considered sneaking out of the service, but our seating choice would have made our early exit awkward.

"I'm a passionate person!" The youth pastor began.

"Everything I do; I do it passionately."

"I was a passionate partier."

He continued to explain how he would go to the Gold Coast with his "blokes" to hit on the "girlies" while getting completely "spiffed" (drunk). He ended up losing everything; homeless, living on the beach, an alcoholic and drug addict. After hitting rock bottom, he was ready to end his life.

There was this one night when he was really drunk, and depressed. He wandered aimlessly down the strip in the pouring rain, nobody around, and that's when he heard it, a rumble, prophetic declaration echoing off the shops, pubs and restaurants.

"Today is the day of salvation!"

It was a street preacher. He didn't have time for a street preacher. He already felt guilty enough. But when the preacher saw him, he switched up sermons like a needle being scratched across a vinyl record. Just like that, the preacher began prophesying, and reading him like a novel. The young man broke down weeping, and that night he gave his life to Jesus.

The preacher gave him an opportunity to literally move into a church building. He became the church janitor, he joined their Bible School, and now he was preaching to us, and doing a great job.

This wasn't just a street preacher; he was a rumbler in disguise. He had a script, but he wasn't ruled by it. He had a plan, and yet it was submitted to the Holy Spirit. In a moment's notice he swiftly shifted from his routine into a prophetic word that would reveal Jesus and save a young man's life.

Rumblers have formulas, but they aren't ruled by them.

Rumblers have friends, but they don't perform for them.

Rumblers have an apostolic covering, but it doesn't cap them.

Rumblers do apostolic ministry, but it doesn't define them.

Rumblers have a call, to be the voice in the wilderness, heralding and demonstrating the supernatural power of the coming redeemer and restorer, Christ Jesus.

THE RISE OF THE GUERRILLA RUMBLERS

Guerrilla warfare is a form of irregular warfare in which a small group of combatants including, but not limited to, armed civilians (or "irregulars"), use bizarre means to accomplish their expected outcome. Guerrilla's don't have unlimited budgets or extravagant technology. They have to be mobile, strategic, and be able to withdraw and disappear immediately.

There is a generation being activated who are engaging in irregular behavior. The method is not what's bringing about the victory, but rather the willingness to obey God no matter how ridiculous it might seem. God is raising up forerunners, small groups of underfunded guerilla *supernaturalists* (another word for guerrilla rumbler revivalists) who will be untouchable, and untraceable. This may sound like a movie, but Hollywood has nothing on Heaven.

LACK AND SPIT

In John 9 there was a man who had "lack" of eyesight. Jesus took some spit and mud and solved the man's problem.

Everything you need to get the job done is in your mouth, and under your feet. Address lack, and choose to not be ruled by it.

DISARMING THE F-BOMB

A couple years back I had the honor of hearing radio talk-show host, Dave Ramsey, speak at a conference. He described being at the airport and watching CNN where they were giving the most recent stats, trends and predictions our economy.

Dave explained, "I know the numbers, and I understand the economy, yet at that moment I felt paralyzed by fear. There was no new information that I didn't already know. I couldn't figure out why I was afraid."

Then Dave dropped the F-bomb.

"I don't know where y'all are at with this, but I believe there was a spirit of fear coming off that screen. I believe that there is a spirit of fear on a lot of this media stuff, and I think it's a load of garbage and I believe that we need to turn it off."

The Lord is raising up a generation of rumblers who will fear no evil. They will not make fear-based decisions, they will engage with fear-based theology and they will actually displace fear-induced atmospheres with the presence of the Lord.

There is too much fear in the world, and there is too much fear in the Church. But everything is changing.

SHALOM ON WHEELS

When I was in the business world, part of the sales training involved a session on "How to open the worry box." It's an advanced marketing technique, and here's how it works: You begin at 30,000 feet. Ask a question that is somewhat specific and yet not too personal such as, "Have you heard the statistic that three out of four airbags in a car do not deploy properly? In fact, airbags tend to break more muscles in a person's face than the average car accident itself."

This is a frightening but fictional statistic.

The second question invites the participant into the tragedy of the stat.

"How would that make you feel if *your* children were in a horrible car accident and the airbags didn't deploy?"

You respond, "That would make me terribly angry."

Now the salesman swoops down to 10,000 feet.

"Statistics tell us" - which they don't - "that three out of four lethal car accidents involve a semi truck. If you were to have a head on collision with a semi-truck, do you think you would live to tell about it?"

"Probably not," you reply soberly.

The salesman has now opened your worry box. You are now thinking about dying in a brutal car accident, whereas ten minutes prior, this would have been the last thing on your mind. You're now asking yourself crazy questions. Questions like "How would my wife pay the mortgage? How would my kids afford college? Who would walk my daughter down the aisle on her wedding day?"

The salesman now brings the plane in for the landing.

"Sir, what if I told you that you would never have to worry about any of this?"

"Wow, that would be nice," you embarrassingly admit.

"Sir with the new Mercedes CL-Class Coupe, I can assure you that neither you, nor your family, will ever die in an automobile accident – unless, of course - the accident involves a 747 jetliner. Sir, if you will just step over here, I will get the paperwork started." And, just like that, your worry box is closed, and it only cost you $115,300.00.

You didn't just buy a Mercedes. You bought shalom on wheels.

Shalom is the Hebrew word for peace. The problem that we Westerners face when we hear the word "peace" is that we immediately think about a ceasefire between countries. Even though that's certainly an important part of peace, when the Hebrews say "shalom" they are referring more than just a season without war. The word shalom means:

Peace, harmony, wholeness, completeness, prosperity, welfare and tranquility and can be used idiomatically to mean both hello and goodbye.

Shalom is the way that things ought to be.

The particular sales training that I engaged with essentially taught us to exploit the default human condition – which is fear - and then solve the crisis by offering them a product, our version of Shalom. Products eventually rust or become outdated; they do not solve the deepest riddles of the soul. Shalom is a person. He is the mystic secret of the ages, He is Christ Jesus, and He dwells within you.

The rumble begins inside of you. It's the voice, the roar, within your soul and spirit that says, "Somebody needs to do something."

The rumble resonates with creation's demand for justice and the cry for the manifested sons of God to be revealed.

The rumble is Heaven's response to religion's inability to meet the needs of our culture and the eternal desires within man's heart.

The rumble is the Earth's response to Heaven as it instigates change upon the face of the Earth.

THE SCIENCE BEHIND HORROR MOVIES

When cruising through movies on NetFlix or RedBox, do you ever wonder why there are so many horror movies? In 2012, Horror films grossed over $413 million, which goes to show that Americans have a fear addiction. Fear sells and doesn't discriminate. If I go to Barnes and Noble, I will find best-selling-fear-provoking books in every category from Christian books to Business books.

Horror movies will continually make boatloads of cash, and will always have international audiences because they systematically open and close the worry box of the audience.

In a dark theater the audience is exposed to mystery and cruelty beyond normal human experience. The audience puts themselves in the character's shoes. They subject themselves to unbearable psychological stress, and yet for over ninety-minutes the responsibilities and chaos of life are forgotten. For a moment in time, there are no more marriage problems, no issues at work, no family conflict, and no more bills that need to be paid.

The audience screams. Characters are murdered at a frequency that is almost comical. Every soul, in every seat, is relieved because they know that this is as bad as it gets, and they are thankful that this isn't their life. This thankfulness shifts the tension. They are no longer a part of the plot but are now safely removed to be a spectator. The movie isn't so scary anymore. It's euphoric. At this point endorphins are being released into the bloodstream and the audience is now high on horror. They have escaped the horror of real life by being exposed to simulated horror on a screen. The audience leaves the theater feeling good and grateful. The audience has just been re-balanced.

The high will last about as long as any other buzz, and will be long gone by the time their buzzing alarm clock sounds the next morning. That's when the real horror continues.

What kind of world pays hundreds of millions of dollars, every year, to subject themselves to simulated terror? The kind of world that desperately needs a pattern interrupt.

HOW TO READ A TERROR METER

I left my television on so I could catch the news while cooking some lovely curry chicken. I quit stirring when I heard Tom Brokaw announce, "We are now code orange." It sounded serious, but I couldn't remember if orange meant we were under attack, or at high risk of attack. If we were at code orange now, what were we yesterday? I searched on Google to find out if the color orange should terrify me. I found the chart. Maybe you will find it helpful.

Code Green = "low risk of attacks."
Code Blue = "guarded risk of attack."
Code Yellow = "elevated risk of attacks."
Code Orange = "high risk of attacks."
Code Red, well, let's not talk about code red.

You will quickly see that there is no code black, and there should be. Code Green should be Code Pink because pink communicates safety, but Homeland Security didn't consult with me before going ahead with their color wheel.

Our country has acclimatized to fear quite well. The media continually reminds us that we have an enemy who hates us, who wants us dead, and is continually devising ways of destroying us. We hear these promises of inevitable terror, and the threats literally go in one ear and out the other. We've learned how to live with our worry box wide open. Products, politicians, and pharmaceuticals all promise to close it, but fail, leaving us frustrated, and feigning for some grade A hope.

²Timothy 1:6-7 says " *For this reason I remind you to fan into flame the gift of God, which is in you through the laying on of my hands, ⁷for God gave us a spirit not of fear but of power and love and self-control.* "

It's possible for a generation to raise up a standard against fear, because God has not given us a spirit not of fear. The Father is raising up rumblers who will displace fear, first in the Church and then in the world.

The spirit of adoption is inviting us to close our worry boxes. No longer will people, places, or things exploit you and drive you to false idols. Whatever has the ability to open our worry box has the ability to control us. All a false god can offer us is temporary and fleeting hope; but any hope that is short-lived is no hope at all.

When we talk about closing the worry box we are referring to the need to intentionally enter into a new level of surrender and consecration to the Lord. When we give the enemy a foothold within our hearts we are actually giving him a key to the back door of our soul.

PATTERN INTERRUPT FOR WORRY

1. Impartation

   Paul encourages us to fan the flame within our hearts. It's a gift of God that's activated through the laying on of hands. This communicates the need for community, submission, and healthy apostolic cultures that are empowering and externally focused. Interrupt worry by engaging in dynamic community and being transparent.

2. Release

   The spirit of power will obliterate the spirit of fear. Release resurrection power against your doubts, concerns, and worries. When the power of God is demonstrated, we see a visible demonstration of the Lord's willingness to engage with our affairs and despair. God is not only *able* to overcome your biggest fears, He is *willing*.

3. Receive

   The spirit of love and self–control will demolish worry. Worrying robs us of the ability to receive the Father's love and give it away. When we worry we actually become self-consumed and even self-obsessed. We can overcome worry by placing our concerns at His feet and receiving His love, and then giving it away to others. Ask the Lord to give you the spirit of self-control to overcome the chaos that's associated with worrying.

4. Volunteer

Being generous with your time and passion is a great pattern interrupt for worry. Sometimes, we have too much time with ourselves. Volunteering doesn't just have to occur at your church, even though that's certainly a good option. You can volunteer at a library, community center, for your city, and local community events. You'll feel a part of something bigger, you'll get an opportunity to be salt and light, and you'll stop worrying. It's a win/win.

WE HAVE A PILL FOR THAT

I have nothing against pharmaceuticals, but I have a beef with pharmaceutical evangelism. Marketers have learned to exploit the human condition. They know about the Eden tragedy, and humanities fear, pessimism, secrecy, insecurity, shame and doubt.

Commercials and magazine ads aim to exploit the void. They show what life could be like if we just took their little purple pill, daily.

Pharmaceutical commercials aren't mere commercials; they are words of knowledge.

Do you avoid confrontation? Are you excessively tired in the morning lacking drive and motivation? Do you feel exhausted trying to carry an overwhelming sense of lack of purpose, identity, and meaning? How would you like to be assertive, driven, inspired, confident, and drop dead sexy?! The makers of Exlax bring you Redbullodone.

The human condition seeks escape without consequences. The request is simple, "Give me a pill that can help me cope." The problem is, cope is simply hope deferred. Cope says, "A pill a day will keep the darkness away."

Cope is the ability to keep a relatively optimistic perspective while living in hell, whereas hope is the un-relentless anticipation of God's intoxicating pleasure. When you look into the Heavens, you'll see hope, not cope.

Is there something that you are doing that is keeping you from a pattern interrupt? Are you intentionally delaying your healing by engaging with hope deferred? Are there relationships, habits, the overindulgence of substances/entertainment, etc., where the spirit of cope is keeping you from engaging with the true spirit of hope?

Religion is just a set of coping behaviors and philosophies that will keep you just busy enough so that your bondage isn't as noticeable. Relationship with Jesus is a dynamic pattern interrupt that will release hope into every area of your life and then radiate through your life into the lives of others.

Rumblers are ambassadors of hope, heralds of hope, and they possess the power of hope. They are gospel-centered, in that their hope is centered in Christ alone. Their mission is to subvert the spirit of cope with the spirit of Christ Jesus, which is our everlasting hope of glory.

Rumblers are not waiting for hope to come, they rumble from a revelation that their hope has come, and is in them.

THE DAVID GENERATION

The story of David and Goliath is an example of God's supernatural strength being flexed through human weakness. A child can't normally kill a heavily armed giant, but he knew that God was for him. Through this child God, restored hope to an unbelieving nation. David was a believer in his God. David was a rumbler.

God wasn't about to be mocked on David's clock. He prophesied to Goliath what would happen if he didn't back down.

"Goliath, even though I am about to kill you, your death in-and-of-itself will not satisfy the demand for justice. Once you have fallen I will saw through your neck with your very own sword - severing your head from your body - then I will kill all of your men and turn their corpses into bird food. Your blood will testify to all the earth the majesty and supremacy of Israel's God. Then everyone will know that the LORD does not save by natural means like swords and spears; for the battle *is* the LORD's, and He will supernaturally give you into our hands."

There were soldiers who were better qualified than David, but they weren't available. Their fear had deemed them powerless. Willingness is a more important than mere ability. When possible, both are preferred.

In times past, the church blazed forward with tremendous power, but little skill. More recently the Western church has advanced with tremendous excellence, but perhaps it's been to overcompensate for possessing little power.

As this generation pursues the things of God, it is critical that we forsake not the power of God for the excellence of man. The two can be held in tension, but the agenda of Heaven must always prevail.

John 3:8 says, "The wind blows where it wishes, and you hear its sound, but you do not know where it comes from or where it goes. So it is with everyone who is born of the Spirit."

The uncontrollable wind-like nature of the Spirit of the Lord is returning to the Church.

2 Chronicles 16:9 says "For the eyes of the LORD run to and fro throughout the whole earth, to give strong support to those whose heart is blameless toward him…" God is actually searching the earth to find a people whom he can support.

We are not qualified by our giftedness but rather by our willingness. There will be many competent people who should engage in this hour, but are not able to because of their fear.

There have been too many Goliaths and not enough Davids, but that's about to change.

PATTERN INTERRUPT FOR PASSIVITY

1. Fear no evil, for the Lord is with you.

2. Confront the problems that exist now in the present, so that you are postured to finish well.

3. Stop apologizing (to man) and start repenting (to the Lord).

4. Stop hiding; complaining in private, and start doing something, in public.

5. Don't take silence for an answer, because it's not.

6. You're a David, so say something, do something, and ENGAGE!

3 DIRECTIVES:

1. Find problems without solutions and look for the opportunities; champion the problems.

2. Find your tribe.

3. Celebrate the big wins.

   - Celebrate the little wins (even more).

SMALL GROUP DISCUSSION QUESTIONS:

- If the Lord let you engineer a revival what would it look like?

- What Goliaths in your life have you found to be the most intimidating, have you been able to defeat them?

ACTIVATION PRAYER:

I declare that I am a rumbler, a mover and a shaker. I am a catalyst for awakening and revival.

I declare that the Lord loves me too much to leave me alone. I am in a season of transformation and growth. I am not stagnant. I am not stuck. I am part of a movement, and His spirit is moving in and through me.

I declare that I am willing to enter into the conflict. I am not afraid. Yesterday's defeat will not keep me from today's victory. The Lord has trained my hands for battle and I will not back down.

I declare that it is no accident that I am at where I am at. I am surrounded by opportunity. I am dripping in favor.

I declare revival and awakening over my family, over my church, over my business and over my region.

I declare that because of me, God will be glorified.

I declare that I will be present. I will be generous. I will be gracious. I will be grateful.

I declare that from this day forward, I will fear no evil.

I declare my role and responsibility to prepare the way for the return of the Lord.

Amen.

7
THE PRESENCE DRIVEN LIFE

The Secret to Liberation

"Now the Lord is the Spirit, and where the Spirit of the Lord is, there is freedom."

- 2 Corinthians 3:17

THE UNITED STATES OF EPHESUS

"Good job guys!"

That was the voice of Jesus. He continued cheerfully, "I know about you; your work ethic, your patient endurance, your commitment to integrity, your keen discernment, and your all around stellar example."

On one hand, he was proud of the Church of Ephesus: they were absolutely nailing it. They could literally check off all the things they were supposed to be doing. They had achieved optimum performance by continually achieving their Kingdom purposes, and yet on the other hand, they had failed miserably. Revelation 2:4-5 tells us that Jesus had one serious complaint, and it was a deal breaker. Somewhere along the way they had fallen out of love with Him. The church was already fighting the tempting allure of institutionalism, and Constantine hadn't even gotten his hands on her yet. This letter was a pattern interrupt. It was Jesus fighting for the heart of His bride, and He wanted for nothing more than to keep intimacy alive.

We, like Ephesus, are nailing it. The Church has never been so family friendly and versatile. Pastors can preach at their pulpit via a prerecorded 3D hologram, and kids can catch a log ride down a man-made river to children's church. I don't think the 1ˢᵗ century synagogues delivered caramel fraps to your seat during worship. Indeed, we've come a long way and yet we've lost something. We, like Ephesus, without question, have lost our first love, but unlike Ephesus we are different in that at least they were walking in the supernatural power of God.

Jesus didn't take kindly to the folks who decided to convert the temple into a Wal-Mart. In His anger and broken heartedness He rebuked their ignorance in forgetting the temple's true purpose: to be a house of prayer for all nations.

Today, Jesus is visiting some places. He's flipping over some tables. He's firing some pastors. He's shutting some places down. He's not impressed with man's efforts to attempt to finish in the flesh what He started in the spirit. His promise was that He would build His Church and the gates of hell would not prevail against it. The Church is experiencing a massively disruptive pattern interrupt. It's necessary for several reasons, including the problem.

THE PROBLEM

Statistics say that the American protestant church has a serious problem. We are shrinking. Not only are we not making new converts, but we're losing old coverts; if they're not backsliding, they're dying of old age. According to the Pew Research Center, surveys conducted in the first half of 2012 reported that fewer than half of American adults say they are Protestant (48%), an all-time low. The fastest growing religion in America is now the "unaffiliated" category. While the Church seems to think that the world wants is relevant programing, the research shows that the "unaffiliated" category of non-churchgoers or "nones" are actually hungry for the supernatural. The "nones" have a fascination with spiritual energy in objects (like trees, mountains and crystals), astrology, reincarnation, Yoga (as a spiritual practice), claim to have had mystical experiences, claim to have been in touch with someone who has died, seen or been in the presence of a ghost, and consulted with a psychic. The fastest growing religion in America is a group of people who are starving for something that will stimulate and feed their spirits, and so they are actively engaging in the demonic realm. The bottom line, <u>the Church has become too secular for the world.</u>

TELL ME WHAT YOU WANT, WHAT YOU *REALLY REALLY* WANT?

The fact that people don't want to go to Christian churches is not the problem in and of itself. We can't just keep adapting our methodology in order to fill seats. Christianity isn't ultimately about church growth, it's about Christ. We can't just do research in order to discover what the un-churched would like to see in a church. We've been there, done that. It was called the 90's, and the *seeker sensitive movement.*

Empty seats, statistics, and even the climate of our culture are indicators of a problem, and at some point, someone is going to have to answer the question, "How do we get back to our first love?" Sure, we'd all love to see our churches packed out on Sunday, but a full church doesn't really mean anything. How full is your heart, and how full is the Father's heart because of the generosity of your heart?

In Matthew 7:22-23, Jesus says that on the day of judgment there will be many who try to remind the Lord of everything they did for him, including supernatural exploits like prophesying, casting out demons and "mighty works," but Jesus says that they will be rejected because they aren't known by Him.

What does Jesus want? He wants you. He wants your heart. He wants to be friends, and He wants to partner with you and do really cool stuff for the Kingdom of God. He wants for you to be absolutely satisfied in Him. He wants to publically display His affection for you, and He wants for you to go public in your affection for Him. He wants you to trade your tradition for spontaneity, and your formulas for intimacy.

He wants to be the Lord of your life, and to reveal Himself through you.

Get ready, because, He's about to jump out and startle you.

BOO!

It all began with a warning, like a blaring hurricane siren from Heaven. It was a new year, two thousand and sixteen, and God wanted my attention. It was a warning that I heeded and even repeated but didn't really know what to do with.

He said he was going to startle me.

I pictured myself walking down a hallway and the Lord waiting around the corner, giggling to Himself, waiting for me to naively make the turn, only to jump out, grab me, and yell, "BOO!"

And that's exactly what He did, He startled me, He yelled, "BOO!" Even with the warning, I nearly peed myself. I remember lying in bed, staring at ceiling and thinking, "Oh God, what are you doing? I hope this is you." My world felt like it had been turned into a milkshake. Everything just got chopped up. In one hand, I like milkshakes, on the other hand, I had a crazy brain freeze and a straw jammed up my nose. It was awesome, but let's rewind a bit.

At the beginning of 2016, God spoke to me and said that we were doing a good job stewarding a local church, but He had called us to be a revival center. I didn't really know what that meant, but it sounded cool. I wanted to make sure that our leadership team was all on the same page and so went on a retreat and discussed revival center practicalities. Little did we know, as we brainstormed through revival philosophies and methodologies, God was jumping out and startling Jerame and Miranda Nelson in San Diego, "BOO!"

Revival is a pattern interrupt: a sovereign and Heavenly intervention into man's systems and routines. Revival is the Spirit of Christ Jesus, loosed upon a people that awakens a loyalty to the pursuit of the Spirit's leadership. We all agree that there has to be more to church life than just events that fill seats; brain food that's Biblically based, and makes us better citizens. There is!

Jesus is jumping out everywhere, and startling all kinds of people. Over the next few pages I'll tell you our story and I'll contrast the difference between the purpose driven life and the presence driven life, and then you can choose for yourself the kind of life you want to live. I think this conversation deserves a conscious choice, a decision. Will we continue to engage in a consumer-based form of Christianity or will we choose to hold nothing back and engage in a company of believers who are being led by the all-consuming fire?

THE WEST COAST RUMBLE

James Goll gave a prophetic word to Jerame and Miranda Nelson, that they would be catalysts in spearheading a move of God known as the *West Coast Rumble*. He prophesied that it would begin in San Diego and move all the way to Vancouver, BC. Little did he know that the

Nelsons would be hosting a conference with Bobby Conner and Joshua Mills called the Decree Conference in San Diego in January of 2016.

When we returned from our retreat we learned about the Decree Conference, and how it had moved to extended meetings. Jerame reported that the presence of God showed up in a powerful way, crazy miracles were happening nightly and so they decided to extend the meetings. People began flying to San Diego from all over the world to experience the spirit of revival. A team of leaders from Seattle Revival Center decided to go and receive a fresh impartation from the Lord.

THE APPLE WINE AWAKENING

On February 13th, 2016, Jerame asked for our team visiting San Diego to stand so he could pray for them. Here is what he said:

"Washington Stand.

In worship the Lord began to show me a massive Apple in the Spirit. I said, God what is that? He said, 'It is what I am releasing, I am releasing the Apple Wine in Washington.' He said, 'In Seattle, Washington, in the northern part of the country, in the northern part of the West Coast, the Apple Wine is going to flow from the Mountain of God. I see the New Wine of Heaven coming and I see God releasing a Fresh Marking, a Fresh Release of the peace of God, of the intimacy of God, the Apple of Your Eye Anointing that He is going to release over the state of Washington and over Seattle, Washington.'

I also see the firestorm moving in and moving out and moving in and moving out and the Lord is marking you today with New Wine in the

Glory. He is marking you today with the Apple of His Eye anointing of intimacy with God and I see the peace of God being released right now - the peace that surpasses all understanding being released in Jesus' name!"

The team came back from San Diego rocked. Pastor Greg Daley preached that following Sunday on the Apple Wine anointing and revival broke out in our 9 AM service. It was loud and crazy. It happened again in our 11 AM service.

I received prayer from the team in both services. As I lay on the ground with my eyes, shut I took in the sound, the roar; it was amazing. I hit the record button on my phone because I wanted to capture the audio. It had been such a long time since I had heard this sound.

I whispered to the Lord, "Don't leave."

He replied, "There's no end to my goodness."

February 21st, 2016

KEEP ON DANCING

The lanterns were lit as the sun set on the horizon, and with the new ambiance came a fresh wind of excitement. The music seemed louder, as did the conversation and laughter. More people moved to the dance floor, whole families sang with glee, and everywhere you looked were manifestations of love and joy. This was how the Hebrew's did weddings; they seemed to invite the whole city. Even Jesus and His disciples had been invited. They reclined at their tables, their wine glasses were about empty. Jesus motioned to one of the hired servants, requesting that His glass be attended to, but the boy's face looked nervous. The boy shook his head as if saying no, and nodded over towards the food and preparation tent. Jesus glanced over and noticed the commotion, and hands flailing in the air. Something was going on, and people were getting worked up. He looked over at the bride and the groom who were dancing and singing amongst a crowd of laughing children. They had no idea of the drama that was going down, it was better that way. Just then something caught Jesus' attention. It was his mom, Mary, she looked distraught and she was making a B-line right for Jesus.

Jesus smiled at his mom, as if trying to calm her down, "What's going on?"

"They are out of wine!"

All the disciples looked at each other as if doubting the validity of what Mary had just said. This was an unthinkable mistake. Either Mary had her facts wrong, someone hadn't planned accordingly, or everybody was drinking way too much wine.

Jesus responded, "Mom, this isn't my problem. I can't really do anything because my time hasn't yet come."

Mary literally ignores Jesus. She looks at his disciples and says, "Do whatever he tells you."

In the natural, this wedding would be ruined and brought to an end by the absence of wine. When the wine was gone, the wedding celebration would end and everybody would go home. Mary wasn't going to allow this celebration to end on her watch because of a lack of wine. She immediately turned to her son. Isn't it interesting that the first miracle of Jesus wasn't instigated by his Heavenly father, but rather by his earthly mother, and she didn't ask?

Biblically wine is symbolic for joy and celebration. Isn't it significant to think that the very first miracle of Jesus, involved turning menial water into top-shelf royal wine. There wasn't a person at that wedding who could have afforded the wine that Jesus created that day, neither was there anyone who deserved to drink such a high caliber and quality vintage.

John 2:9-11 says, "[9]When the master of the feast tasted the water now become wine, and did not know where it came from (though the servants who had drawn the water knew), the master of the feast called the bridegroom [10]and said to him, "Everyone serves the good wine first, and when people have drunk freely, then the poor wine. But you have kept the good wine until now." [11]This, the first of his signs, Jesus did at

Cana in Galilee, and manifested his glory. And his disciples believed in him."

If only we could be like Mary; not willing for a party to end, nor willing to settle for dry religious events. Most feast masters serve the best wine first, and then once people are good and drunk they bring out the box wine, but who is this God who actually saves the best for last? The best is yet to come in your life! You have permission to seek the wine; the joy, and the kind of intimacy that can only be found in His presence. You have permission to find enjoyment and satisfaction in Him. Your celebration doesn't have to end, or for some of you, a time of celebration can actually begin.

LET'S KEEP GOING

The next weekend - after our team returned home from San Diego – was our prophetic conference with Bobby Conner that we call Declaration Conference. This year, Patricia King, Leif Hetland and Charlie Shamp were also joining us. It was so interesting because Jerame's conference was called Decree and also featured Bobby Conner, and just like Decree, the presence of the Lord showed up, and miracles started popping like Pringles containers.

Charlie Shamp came to speak at a three-day conference and stayed for five weeks. We began hosting extended meetings and with those meetings came a wave of signs, wonders, creative miracles, glory manifestations, deliverances, salvations and water baptisms. We saw manifestations of the full gospel. People were literally being healed, delivered, saved, water baptized and filled with the Holy Spirit all within a 24 – 72 hour span. In the first four weeks we saw three stage-four doctor-verified cancer healings, forty plus decisions and re-dedications for Christ and thirty-two water baptisms. Imagine three years' worth of fruit harvested in thirty days; that's what God did. Every day my phone was blowing up with text messages and emails of miracles, testimonies, and reports of extended meetings within the region. The glory of God was moving like a firestorm. Indeed, revival was in the air.

MY PRESENCE IS THE PURPOSE

The atmosphere was thick with the presence of the Lord and so I did what any reasonable pastor would do, I laid down. Waves of His presence began to crash over me with unusual frequency and duration. Tears streamed down my face like a beautiful Hawaiian waterfall. From my nostrils flowed a torrent that resembled that of Niagara Falls (not as beautiful). I was coming undone, becoming one with the mint green carpet underneath me, and that was unusual considering it was a Sunday morning.

I inquired of the Lord, "What are you doing to me?" I just wanted to confirm that He wasn't trying to drown me. I couldn't discern what He was doing, or what He was fixing, or healing. It felt incredible and yet I couldn't figure out what the purpose of it all was. I thought maybe He was going to download a crazy revelation, a new message for the morning, and so I waited and waited, and then He spoke, "Darren, why do you need a purpose for my presence? Why can't my presence be the purpose?"

I felt so convicted. I was trying to siphon a preachable message out of an encounter with the Father. He was just responding to my heart's cry to come close, and once He answered my prayer with His presence, it wasn't enough; I had to figure out His motive. Then He continued, "Darren, why can't you just enjoy me, for me?"

"I'm so sorry," I replied, and then I wept some more.

Revival, awakening, outpouring, inpouring, renewal, and transformation, it's all about one thing: HIM. We mustn't get in a hurry. When God shows up, we must slow down, and if necessary even stop everything. When the King walks into the room, it's important that we follow proper protocol. When our God is so incredibly generous with His presence, how can we not but drop everything, just to stare into His eyes.

There are too many Christian scientists in the Church; too many theories and hypothesis. There is too much analyzing and not enough Son gazing. Jesus came so that we could have abundant, flourishing, vibrant and colorful life. The dream of God for you is that you would live your life so intoxicated in the wine of His peace and love that He could use your childlikeness to reveal the mystery, beauty, power and authority of the Kingdom.

Psalm 37:4 says, "Delight yourself in the LORD, and he will give you the desires of your heart." This is a commandment. The command is to delight ourselves: to receive joy, satisfaction, and peace directly from

Him. As we've already learned, God isn't glorified through our religious striving, but He's actually worshiped through our willingness to drink deep of the satisfying pleasures of God. When we have the courage to find our satisfaction in Him, the psalmist tells us that our satisfaction actually unlocks the dreams and desires of our hearts. So, ditch the agenda from your intimacy, and delight yourself in the Lord, drink deeply, and be satisfied in Him.

Receiving and enjoying the presence of the Lord isn't greedy or selfish; in fact, one of the most important ways that we can demonstrate love is by having the humility to receive love. When love cannot be received, intimacy begins to break apart like a weathered sandcastle. When all we do is give, give, give, we may think that we are demonstrating love but it may actually be a greater demonstration of control. We cannot stay emotionally healthy without learning how to receive good and perfect gifts from our Father of Lights. Refusing to receive will leave us chronically empty, prone to addiction, obsession, codependency, and an eternal hunger of the soul that will remain unsatisfied.

There's no better way to surrender control than to receive a gift from the Lord. A gift from the heart has a way of disarming us. It humbles us. It makes us confront the parts of our heart that are hidden and don't want to be seen. The heart starts asking questions like, "Can I trust again?"

Traumatic experiences and disappointments have a way of putting us into cruise control - where we cruise fast and hard while taking complete control. It is time to stop cruising, it is time to surrender control, and it is time to confront the pain of the past and to begin receiving healing from our Father so that the real us can emerge.

As you can see, I am still learning how to be ministered to by the Lord without going into ministry mode. I am learning how to be loved by the Lord without running immediately into some sort of love performance. I am learning how to enjoy His presence without trying to find the hidden agenda behind His presence. I am learning how to emerge and find my confidence within my sonship. I am becoming a better receiver.

FRAME A MOVE

Did you know that historically, most revivalists didn't even recognize that they were in the midst of revival until it was over? Even William Joseph Seymour, in the midst of the Azusa Street revival was looking to the future, to that which the Lord was going to do, while not realizing the impact of what God was doing in the present. Most of us fail to celebrate the present because we are addicted to the future. God Himself could descend and walk down the aisle of our churches, in bodily form, and most of us would say, "Someday, God is going to do something really crazy."

America is in a Genesis 28:16-17 moment, "[16] Then Jacob awoke from his sleep and said, "Surely the LORD is in this place, and I did not know it." [17] And he was afraid and said, "How awesome is this place! This is none other than the house of God, and this is the gate of heaven."

AMERICA, THE LORD IS IN YOUR MIDST AND YOU DO NOT KNOW IT!

Please stop groaning and panting, screaming for God to come. He's here, and He will freely move through a company of people who will believe. The hardest thing for a believer to do is believe, but for the one who dares to believe, God will show up and demonstrate His power.

Revival doesn't just happen. It takes a Peter-like leader to frame a move. In Acts 2:16 Peter goes before the people and frames up what God was doing in the upper room; Peter had the audacity to say what no one else would, "This is that!" I want to be this kind of leader. I want to prophetically frame moves of God across the Earth. I want to instigate belief, and unlock regions to their true potential. I want to judo chop fear in the gut, and trigger religious spirits. I want to be like Peter, declaring to my generation, "This is that!" This is the moment the prophet Joel prophesied. This is the moment Peter prophesied. This is the moment Jesus prophesied. This is the moment Smith *stinkin* Wigglesworth prophesied.

So, no, you aren't waiting on God. He's waiting on you. It's time to engage. Go ahead and host extended meetings, you've got my permission. You don't need a visitation from angel Gabriel to do so. Celebrate EVERY little testimony and answered prayer on Facebook, Periscope, Twitter, and Instagram. Get the word out. Don't be shy. Put an ad in your local paper, "GOD IS REAL AND WE CAN PROVE IT!" Use your creative breath to frame a move of God in your region and in your generation. Be the leader you've always wanted to see emerge. Be original, create a ruckus, and lean into the awkwardness. In times like these we need true leaders who will not rely on their own giftings, charisma, and PowerPoint's, but rather walk in a vibrant demonstration of the Spirit of Power.

DON'T LET THIS REVOLUTION PASS YOU BY

If you're waiting for something to happen, you're missing out. There is a revival occurring in the remnant. We are no longer on the verge; we've been pushed over the edge. There's no going back - just an invitation from the Lord to enter into a deeper place of mystery and intimacy.

If you're contending for revival in a church that doesn't value revival, you're wasting your time. Every church has its own DNA, and Kingdom assignment, and so don't use your influence, leadership and gifts to be divisive in a church. We don't have permission to use our prayers to enforce our will on others. Your pastor needs the freedom to fulfill his call without feeling pressure (from you) to have to be the next Bill Johnson.

Know what's in your scroll and take responsibility for that. Your call should determine the community that you're running with. Unless otherwise directed by the Holy Spirit, I would encourage you to find an apostolic community that will partner with you, to see you come into your fullness.

We are in a season of reformation and revolution, and this movement begins with you and me. We have to become a people of the Spirit; filled with the Spirit, led of the Spirit, and full of the fruit of the Spirit. What God is doing right now is crazy! Count the cost, hold nothing back, and don't let this revolution pass you by.

3 DIRECTIVES:

1. Evaluate your scene: Are you plugged into a crew that loves, values, and guards the presence of the Lord?

2. Evaluate your heart: Have you become process-driven at the expense of forgetting about Him?

3. Evaluate your time: Are you actively engaging with His presence and growing in Him?

SMALL GROUP DISCUSSION QUESTIONS:

- What are some ways that your home group could become more presence-driven?

- Does your group engage in worship or soaking prayer? If not, is there a way that you can begin to incorporate these elements into your group?

- What part of "God showing up" frightens you?

ACTIVATION PRAYER:

I declare I am a temple of the Holy Spirit.

I have been created to hold His glory, and so I declare that I am absolutely full of the glory of the Lord.

His nation-changing power is residing within me, transforming me, from the inside out.

I declare I am an image bearer of the Lord, and I have surrendered my life so as to reflect the beauty, truth and majesty of the Lord.

I declare that I do not fear man's opinion of me. I know that I am loved and infinitely valued therefore I can host His presence well.

I declare that I am open to the new things that Heaven has for the Earth.

I am not stuck in the past. I am anchored to Him. Where he goes I will go. I'm ready to move as He leads me.

I declare that I am capable of releasing His presence into the Earth.

I am a gateway.

I say, "yes" to my responsibility to reveal the government of His peace upon the Earth.

I declare that my authority is in Him.

I am a person of authority; an ambassador and diplomat of redemption and restoration.

I say, "yes" to the presence of the Lord and His plans and purposes for my life and generation.

Amen.

8

I'M SORRY, YOU'RE GOING TO HAVE TO LEAVE

Displacing the Demonic

"When the unclean spirit has gone out of a person, it passes through waterless places seeking rest, but finds none. ⁴⁴ Then it says, 'I will return to my house from which I came.' And when it comes, it finds the house empty, swept, and put in order."

– Matthew 12:43-44

TRACY'S GHOST

There it was again, thuds and creaking. Tracy looked over at the alarm clock that sat on the nightstand next to her bed. It was 2:30AM. She quickly pulled the blankets over her head as a cold shiver shuttered down her spine. Pieces of drywall began to fall like snow as nails began popping out of the ceiling. "Something just ain't right," Tracy, a single mother of five, told the *Charlotte Observer,* "I thought that there was some poltergeist stuff going on." When her adult sons went up to confront the ghost, they found Tracy's ex-boyfriend asleep in the back of the attic. He had been released from jail two weeks prior and had turned the attic into an apartment. Police found his attic toilet - "Route 44" Sonic cups – apparently filled with feces and urine. The only way into the attic was through was through a door inside the home. When confronted he shot up to his feet, he jetted past Tracy's sons, out of the attic, through one of the kid's bedrooms, down the stairs and out the door before the police could arrive. The suspect is still at large.

Tracy thought that she had ended the relationship, and technically she had, but the ex-lover still felt entitled to her domain.

This is all too common. Post-breakup cohabitating. You say, "I dealt with that years ago. We are over." Then why is it there, living in your house, and eating your favorite dark chocolate out of your pantry?"

Sometimes we get unwanted visitors who have no intent to ever leave. Sometimes they are sneaky and live in the attic, and sometimes they are obvious and sleep in plain sight on our living room couch.

The question begs to be asked. Once you know this uninvited guest is living in your home, what will it take before you kick it out?

TOO MUCH POOP COFFEE

My cell phone vibrated, informing me that I had received a text message. I discreetly pulled it out my pocket. There was a picture of my dad, white as a sheet, head dangling, and drool hanging out of his mouth. He looked dead.

I played it cool. I had a special guest teaching my class and so I snuck out the back door without causing too much commotion.

Just then I got another picture, and then another. They were getting worse. In one picture he was laying on the floor, and in another they had him strapped to a stretcher. Then I received a message, "Hi!

Darren. You dad fell out of chair while he eating. He has heart attack. You come get him?"

I quickly responded, "Is he okay? Please send me your phone number so I can call you."

They texted me a phone number and so I called Indonesia. They put my dad on the phone - which was a bit awkward considering he was having a heart attack and couldn't speak. There was nobody with him who could speak English and Google translator only works for written words.

I could hear him breathing.

"Dad, is that you?"

He muttered something intangibly.

"Dad, you okay?"

He wasn't able to speak. I told him that I loved him. I prayed a prayer of faith. Then I assured him I'd be staying in the loop.

Then there was about fourteen hours of silence and then we received word that everything was fine; it was a false alarm. Here's what happened.

After an intensive and strenuous travel schedule, my dad went and did a series of revival meetings. With jet lag, little sleep, and meeting adrenaline pumping through his veins he did what any revivalist would do, he proceeded to drink three cups of poop coffee – a highly caffeinated coffee that's roasted after exiting the rectum of an Asian civet, also called a toddy cat. The coffee began to cause heart palpitations at which point my dad popped a Nitro (heart medication pill), he popped another pill after noticing that the first hadn't done the trick. His blood pressure plummeted causing him to pass out. Thinking that he was having a heart attack, one of his pastor friends proceeded to grab the Nitro bottle and feed him additional pills causing his blood pressure to fall even more.

The good news was that his heart was fine. The poop coffee mixed with a bottle of Nitro pills is what almost killed him.

Sometimes there are external factors, demonic factors, that have the ability to trick us into believing that we have a problem, or worse yet, we are the problem. When we misdiagnose what the real problem is, sometimes our solutions do more damage than the problem itself. Before you interrupt a pattern, make sure you've discerned the right problem.

IMPOSTERS MAKE FOR LOUSY LORDS

In Luke 4:25 Jesus rebuked the evil spirit that was possessing the man. The word for rebuke in this text is the Greek word "epetimēsen" which is a very harsh word used to deal with an imposter. Here's where it gets fascinating; Jesus used that same word to rebuke "all sicknesses." In Luke 4:39 "And He (Jesus) stood over her [Simon's wife's mother] and rebuked [epetimēsen— the same word as in Luke. 4: 35] the fever; and it left her."

So Jesus rebuked a demon in the same way that he rebuked a fever.

Acts 10:38 says that Jesus went with the Holy Ghost and with power and "went about doing good, and healing all who were oppressed of the devil; for God was with Him." The word oppressed here is actually the Greek word *Katadunasteuomenous* which means *down or under the power of lordship of.* The Greeks would have understood this word "oppressed" as "under the lordship of Satan."

Jesus treated sickness and disease the same way that he treated demons - harshly. He understood that any violation to a person's wellbeing was a violation against shalom itself, and was therefore an act of demonic injustice. Jesus knew that demonic imposters make for lousy lords. When He would heal the sick, He would actually pull people out from underneath the lordship of the spirit of infirmity.

Sometimes we are far too hospitable with the demonic. Serving fresh coffee and warm blueberry scones to a spirit of heaviness every morning doesn't do anybody any good. It's time to swap out that scone for a Holy Spirit hand grenade. It's time to be done hosting demons who end up just harassing you. It's time to begin hosting the presence of the Holy Ghost.

DEMONS USE DOORS

A demon can't break into you through a locked window. Demons come into our lives through open doors. Examples of open doors include:

- Sin, which is giving Satan an advantage (2 Corinthians 2:10-11)

- Seeking others with occult power (Leviticus 19:31)

- Idol worship (Ezekiel 20:7)

- Cursed objects (Deuteronomy 7:26)

- Bestiality (Leviticus 18:23)

- Sex outside of Biblical marriage, adultery, and homosexuality (Genesis 34:2)

- The power of the tongue (Proverbs 18:21).

COFFEE WITH JESUS

Why not make Jesus some muffins first thing in the morning?! In all seriousness, Jesus doesn't like muffins; He likes coffee; fresh, bold, burnt, bitter coffee; without cream or sugar.

One of the most important principles for getting free and staying free is to begin intentionally hosting the presence of Jesus.

In Psalm 5:3, David says, "O LORD, in the morning you hear my voice; in the morning I prepare (brew) a sacrifice (a pot of coffee) for you and watch." David knew that if he started his day the right way, the rest of the day would prosper. David would begin his day with worship, prayer and coffee. He would center himself in the Lord so that the presence of God would govern within his governing.

When you begin to intentionally host the presence of the Lord, His lordship begins to uproot the lies and lordship of demonic defeater beliefs and influences. As you begin to drink of His presence, He will literally begin to influence your thoughts, decisions and actions. It is possible to begin your day under the influence of His intoxicating affections for you. The easiest way to get delivered is to begin drinking of the wine of His intimacy daily, and specifically, first thing in the morning.

THE SIGNIFICANCE OF 25 MINUTES

When you begin your day by diving down deep into His heart, the surface level storms will not be able to impact you. The demonic can't trigger you when you are hidden within his heart. Just twenty-five minutes a day can keep Satan away.

What's so significant about 25 minutes? Nothing. It's simply a manageable time interval that anybody should be able to incorporate into their busy schedule without having to reorg the whole day. The concept of using manageable time intervals to execute task is called the Pomodoro Technique and was developed by Francesco Cirillo in the late 1980s. Francesco used a timer that looked like a tomato - hence pomodoro, which is Italian for tomato - and broke down his activities into twenty-five-minute time increments separated by short breaks.

POMODORO TECHNIQUE FOR ENGAGING GOD

1. Plan

   Plan your twenty-five-minute quiet time, ahead of time. You may soak in the presence of the Lord with music, or you may choose to meditate on God's Word in silence. This is your time with the Lord. There's no right way or wrong way. The purpose of this time is to quiet your soul and allow for the Lord to speak to you.

2. Time

Set a timer for your quiet time. I use my cell phone. Make sure you put your phone on airplane mode so that you are unable to be distracted by social media, email, or text messages.

3. Journal

Quickly jot down the results of your time with the Lord. Just a line or two will do. Some people love Moleskine journals; I personally use my Evernote app with a Notebook titled "Journal."

I'M GOING TO TAKE YOU TO COURT

I was totally vindicated in my frustration. I had gone past the anger zone into the danger zone. I don't even know what that means except that my blood was boiling. I pulled my car into a parking spot and figured I had better pray. It had come to that.

Just prior to me being triggered, I had a fascinating lunch with my friend Justin Abraham. Justin had been engaging with courtroom prayer for quite some time and I had no idea how it worked or if it worked. For forty-five minutes, I drilled Justin with countless question. I wanted to figure this out.

So there I was, ticked off, and I was about to take this whole mess to court, that is, into the courtroom of Heaven.

"Father, thank you for your presence, your grace, and your forgiveness."

It's Psalm 100:4, "Enter his gates with thanksgiving, and his courts with praise!"

I took my time. The presence of the Lord filled the car.

"Lord, I have no idea what I'm doing. I am an amateur at this."

Then it was repentance time.

"Father I repent for my anger, for…"

I started repenting for all kinds of things. The Holy Spirit actually began reading to me the list of things I needed to repent of. Then I repented for partnering with these spirits, i.e. the spirit of anger, the spirit of passivity, the spirit of etc.

Once I had taken responsibility for my sins and for patterning with these impostors who were living in my attic, I asked my Father, the Judge, to summon them into His courts. Sometime people actually see this happening.

Just like that, BOOM, it was as if He had immediately issued His judgment and ruled on my behalf. The sun instantly came out from behind the clouds and filled my car with light. My burdens immediately lifted. The demons that had been messing with my head were gone, and not only in me, but in the other party as well. Our whole relational dynamic changed immediately. I had just taken myself through deliverance, and it felt great.

YOU'RE NOT ALONE

When faced with opposition, temptation, oppression and something as common as discouragement, don't forget you're not alone, unless you are. Often within the context of community, the attacks of the enemy come against the whole community, and so if you are feeling discouraged, usually that means that there are others who are feeling the same way.

1 Corinthians 10:13 says, "No temptation has overtaken you that is not common to man. God is faithful, and he will not let you be tempted beyond your ability, but with the temptation he will also provide the way of escape, that you may be able to endure it." Paul is basically saying, "Don't think that you are special because you're getting picked on by the enemy, but at the same time, don't lose heart. God is faithful and by His grace you can actually maneuver your way through the flying bullets without getting hit."

Within community you can know that you're not alone, and like a server network, within community there is an opportunity for heightened sensitivity, discernment, and an awareness of Heavenly opportunities. Romans 12 says that the Church is a body composed of members with several diverse functions; together not only are we stronger, but we are sharper.

COMMUNITY AS A PATTERN INTERRUPT

1. Recognize

   With isolation comes restriction and limited opportunity.

2. Forgive

   Be willing to let go of those who have hurt you in the past. Refuse to allow the pain of the past to inhibit you in the present.

3. Remember

   The enemy uses communities to destroy and define, but God uses community to redeem and restore. This goes for family, churches, friends, work environments, etc.

4. Engage

   Engage in a Christ-centered church. Visit: www.isupernaturalist.com/church.html to learn about how to pick, join, and leave a church.

IDENTIFICATION

Imagine you are hosting a party, you're having a good time. A little Def Leppard is serenading the room, and you are snacking away on cheesy weenies. It's the perfect party except for this jerk who keeps bumping into you, spilling food and drinks on you, and perhaps at a certain point he actually begins to scare you. What should you do? You should turn around and look at the *HELLO MY NAME IS* sticker on his chest, address him by name and kick him out.

It's important that we don't blame ourselves for the pressure put upon us by demonic spirits. We must discern and identify who it is exactly that is spilling their food on us and then figure out how they got into the party. Don't blame yourself for being picked on. The fact that you are of Christ makes you a target. You should feel honored when confronted with spiritual warfare.

PARTY CRASHERS

So how did this imposter get into Tracy's attic and into your 80's party? Satan is a legalist. He won't come in unless he has a legal right, meaning, if the door is locked, he can't come in. So, who made it inside the party? Identify the imposter and then close the legal door by taking responsibility for how you may have unintentionally or intentionally partnered with it. Also, you should be aware that these guys usually travel with an entourage, meaning, that like mice, if you see one, there's bound to be more.

Our sin is what opens the doors to these party crashers: un-forgiveness can open the door to bitterness; bitterness can open the door to infirmity, infirmity can open the door to compromise, and so-on, so-forth.

The Holy Spirit will show you the point of origin.

Come into the presence of the Lord with thanksgiving, praise and humility, and seek Him for understanding. Take responsibility for how you have sinned in the past, and repent for partnering with these party crashers. Be thorough, and take your time.

Once you are done, stand before the Lord forgiven, innocent, and covered in his blood. You're Heavenly Father is also the Judge. He will be happy to execute His justice on your behalf.

EVICTION

"Now go! Get out! Scram! Right now, out!" I said, and just like that the lady hit the ground with a scream. Shame, bitterness, guilt, abandonment, all began to flood up and out. She began coughing as if she was going to throw up. This was all perfectly normal, and perfectly healthy. Then the presence of the Lord began to flood over her. She had just experienced the eviction of several imposters who had been living in her attic.

I was recently ministering to a group of high school students at our local park. The power of God was moving and these guys were getting saved, one by one. Then of the larger guys came up to me, no shirt on, flexing his muscles as if trying to intimidate me while staring me down.

"What do you want?" I asked. "You want me to pray for you." He continued staring at me and began to grunt and snarl at me.

"Oh I get it." I said. I recognized *them.*

"Now you listen to me. This young man does not belong to you. He was created by the Lord, and for the glory of God. This young man has been bled for. He's was died for. Now let him go!"

All of a sudden his pecs began flopping all over the place. He jumped back, while grunting and snarling. A loud voice came out, "I am --------- --- the lord of ------------------, and I bla bla bla bla…"

It was all quite spectacular and it was freaking out all the kids who were with him. I kept on him.

"I know who you are, now COME OUT!"

He stumbled into a group of Mormon kids and he began talking to them in another language. The kids immediately grabbed their stuff and bailed out of the park. I kept on him. That's when I noticed a medallion of sorts hanging around his neck.

"Hey bro, look at me. Look at me! I want you to take off that necklace." He grabbed it in his hand and began to take it off when one of the demons forced him to put it back on. The demon then began to explain why he could not remove it.

The eviction was being held up, and my faith was being reduced by the time factor and the demonstrative nature of his manifestations. This was one of the most demonstrative and public encounters I had ever had and at a certain point I began to second-guess myself. I believe I will see him again and I believe he's going to get absolutely set free. I thank God for this amazing learning opportunity, certainly the most significant I have ever had.

The bottom line: Serving an eviction notice to someone else's imposter can be tricky, timely, and can require tremendous perseverance but we have the authority to handle these things, and so I'd encourage you to go after it. Secure your attic and help others get their homes back as well.

INHABITED

[43] "When the unclean spirit has gone out of a person, it passes through waterless places seeking rest, but finds none. [44] Then it says, 'I will return to my house from which I came.' And when it comes, it finds the house empty, swept, and put in order. [45] Then it goes and brings with it seven other spirits more evil than itself, and they enter and dwell there, and the last state of that person is worse than the first. So also will it be with this evil generation." – Matthew 12:43-45

Jesus is saying, if a house is empty long enough, it's just a matter of time until the house is filled again with demonic squatters. It's not enough to just eliminate the presence of the demonic; we must cultivate a flourishing atmosphere for Heaven within our hearts. It's so important that we not only displace the demonic but we actually replace those spirits with the Holy Spirit. You are invited to a great exchange. Give Him your heart of stone and He will give you a heart of flesh; give Him your sorrow and He will give you joy; give Him your anxiety and He will give you rest, and give him your fear and He will give you love.

It's important to specifically identify the exchange. For example, if you've evicted the spirit of greed, declare and replace it with the spirit of cheerful generosity. Engage in an activation and rail against your natural disposition to withhold your finances and make a radical investment as a pattern interrupt offering to the Lord. This is not just a positive affirmation that you are making, or just being mindful of negative behaviors, it's actually dealing with the demonic root behind sin, addressing it, dismantling it, and engaging with the spirit of the Lord within that area of your life.

Surrendering your all to the Lord doesn't just mean that God cleans you out; He actually comes and fills you back up, with Himself. Paul would say it like this in 1 Corinthians 6:19-20, "[19]Or do you not know that your body is a temple of the Holy Spirit within you, whom you have from God? You are not your own, [20]for you were bought with a price. So glorify God in your body."

It's time to no longer tolerate attitudes and behaviors that have traditionally and generationally ruled over us. It's time to pay attention to what manifests within our hearts when we are scared, angry, offended, or sad. It's time for us to get serious about executing justice within our soul life. In order to do this, we must surrender our right to silently judge everybody else's issues, and start taking our own issues far more seriously. The Lord wants to rule on your behalf. It's time to get free.

IT'S ABOUT TO GET REAL

Everybody is inhabited with something or someone because humans aren't robots. We are flesh and blood with a soul and a spirit. The dramatic emphasis of demons in the 80's caused us to swing like a pendulum into the 90's, so far to the right that we almost pretended that there was no demonic realm. With the 2000's has come a spiritualistic openness within the culture to the demonic realm. Sorcery, soul travel, channeling the dead, astral projection, fortune telling, and spiritual cleansing are making a major resurgence with the USA. The religious landscape in America is changing. According to a recent study from the 2014 Pew Research Center, the fastest growing religious group in America are those who have no religious affiliation whatsoever. Since 2007, there has been a 7% decline in the number of people who identify themselves as Christian. The fasting growing religion in America is composed of people who claim to have no religion, and they are referred to as the "nones". For every new convert in America there are four former Christians who have fallen away from Christ. "Nones" now outnumber both Protestant and Catholic groups combined. Here's the deal, only a third of "nones" are actually atheist, the rest are totally open to the supernatural realm. According to the study 30% believe in spiritual energy in physical objects, 30% have felt "in touch" with someone who is dead, 25% believe in astrology and reincarnation, and 15% have consulted with a physic.

With our culture's openness to the demonic realm, there is a new level of demonic influence and oppression. With the increase of these factors has come a new intensity in deliverance. We are starting to see demonic manifestations that are on the same scale as occurrences that would be typical in India or Africa.

COUNTERFEIT GATEWAYS

I'm about to tell you about a demon possessed band that performs exorcisms at their concerts, but first let me tell you about a drug that has to be administered by a witch doctor that will cure you of methamphetamine and heroin addiction. Ibogaine, it's a psychoactive substance found in plants in the Apocynaceae family and is used for ritualistic purposes within African spirituality. Westerners have been taking their drug addicted friends and family members overseas for years to have Ibogaine administered, until more recently, the drug is being illegally administered by "guides" or "sitters", outside of the FDA's blessing. The drug instigates a spiritual journey that involves an end-of-life psychedelic trip; the participant gets to replay their whole life, from birth to death, and even continue into an after-life experience that may involve going to Heaven, Hell, or both. Following the encounter, the subject is usually severely depressed, but with proper oversight from a shaman or witch doctor, the person can be guided back into to a healthy state of mind and will usually never touch drugs again.

Get ready because the witch doctors are coming to, and have already arrived in America. MAPS or Multidisciplinary Association for Psychedelic Studies are raising significant amounts of money to see the use of psychedelics used within mainstream medicine under the care of a proper "guide."

Johns Hopkins University, New York University, University of New Mexico, University of California, Los Angeles (UCLA), and the

University of Zurich, are all investing significant funding and research into the study of Psilocybin, a psychedelic compound produced by more than 200 species of mushrooms as a drug to treat cancer distress and addiction. The Heffter Research Institute is a 501C3 that is partnering with the Universities mentioned above, and exists to spearhead this initiative. Here is their mission statement:

The Heffter Research Institute promotes research of the highest scientific quality with the classic hallucinogens and related compounds (sometimes called psychedelics) in order to contribute to a greater understanding of the mind leading to the improvement of the human condition, and to alleviate suffering.

This organization actually exists to open demonic gateways by which a person can step into a realm where their physical or emotional pain can no longer affect their soul.

While we are being called to engage in Heaven's rumble, Hell is making the same appeal. The outspoken Satanic heavy metal band, Ghost, released their third studio album, *Meliora*, in 2015, to much critical acclaim and staggering high record sales, reaching number one in their home country of Sweden and number eight in the United States. Its lead single, "Circe" earned them the 2016 Grammy Award for Best Metal Performance. This particular song begins with the lyrics:

I feel your presence amongst us

You cannot hide in the darkness

Can you hear the rumble?

Can you hear the rumble that's calling?

The band's vocalist wears a prosthetic face with skull face paint, dresses up like the pope and is referred to as "the demonic anti-Pope." Prophets Bob Jones, Paul Keith Davis, and Bobby Conner have been talking about this for years. There is a wave of darkness that has been released onto the earth, and the earth has received it. Now it's time to clean it up, but we must start with ourselves, as you can't fight darkness with darkness.

Obtaining and maintaining our freedom is a great goal, but it's not the end, as much as it is a means to an end. We are going to need to begin discerning and displacing the demonic corporately, and regionally, and then begin replacing it with the atmosphere of Heaven. We have tolerated the demonic for far too long, and it's time to let the darkness know, "We're sorry, but you are going to have to leave."

3 DIRECTIVES:

1. Identify generational demonic patterns within your family. Write them down. Do your research. Ask questions.

2. Repent, for intentionally or unintentionally partnering with these spirits within these patterns, and ask the Lord to rebuke and judge the spirits on your behalf.

3. Replace their presence with the Holy Spirit and the values that appropriately address the areas of neglect.

SMALL GROUP DISCUSSION QUESTIONS:

• Have you ever been delivered of something? Have you ever walked someone else through the deliverance process?

• Have you ever felt called to deliverance ministry?

• Have you ever stood as a priest before the Lord to see deliverance come to a region by repenting, asking the Lord to judge, and then replacing the demonic with the Word of God?

ACTIVATION PRAYER:

I declare 2 Corinthians 3:17, "Now the Lord is the Spirit, and where the Spirit of the Lord is, there is freedom." I declare that I am a temple made to hold your presence. I declare that Your presence is in me. I have the spirit of liberty at work within my innermost being. I was born to be free and I choose to not tolerate any form of bondage or darkness. I repent for opening the door to the demonic and giving an advantage to Satan. I repent for seeking power outside of the cross. I repent for partnering with the sin of idolatry, and idol worship. I repent for engaging with and hosting cursed objects. I repent of all sexual sin. I repent for using my tongue for evil. I break alliance with every unclean thing. I thank You that I stand forgiven and clean, now Father I ask that You would judge these spirits that I have partnered with. Thank You Father that You are downloading Your desires into my heart and that I have the mind of Christ. Let Your light and glory come and flood every area of my heart where I have hosted darkness and vain imagination. Thank you Father for the discernment to know when one of these creepy crawlies would like to sneak back into my attic. Thank you for purchasing my freedom, with the blood of your Son, my Lord and Savior, Jesus Christ. Amen.

9
REFRAME THE FUTURE

The Power of the Word of God

"By the Word of the Lord were the heavens made and all their host by the breath of his mouth."

- Psalm 33:6 AMP

FEAR BASED SPEECH

"And God said, 'Let there be light,' and there was light," Genesis 1:3. This first act of creation was a decision made by the Lord. It didn't require a vote from a Board of Directors and there was no conversation regarding the liabilities associated with light. When God created light, he simply spoke the desire of His heart, and it manifested, but it didn't end there. For six days, God continued speaking, and with each word, with each breath, more was created, and then on the seventh day, after all had been created, God rested. Creation was a manifestation of the Father's heart; made possible by the spoken word of God.

The ministry of Jesus continued this pattern. In fact, Jesus admits in John 5:19 that He only does what he sees his Father do; in John 12:49 Jesus says that He only speaks what He hears the Father say. His words were loaded with wonder; He was the voice of the Lord upon the Earth. The Father's heart was manifesting a new covenant reality through His surrendered son.

Breath, words, and the tongue are very important Biblically as they have the ability to create, destroy, and frame life, death, success and failure, over others and ourselves. James 3:10 says that both blessing and cursing can be released from the same tongue. When we hear "cursing" we immediately think of swear words, but cursing is the release of word curses: identity-framing words that give power to demonic forces.

Perhaps one of the greatest pattern interrupts needed within the Church concerns our speech. Many Christians release words like a soldier lobs hand grenades, blowing up people's dreams before they're even able to get off the ground. If your heart is full of terror, then you've been compromised.

"This will never work," is a word curse that frames fear over an endeavor. "What's wrong with you, you can't do anything right," is a word curse that frames failure as an inevitable demise. "Everything is your fault," is a word curse that like the others, is rooted in a lie and frames up defeat. When we use phrases like these, we might as well be cooking up a witch stew out of frog legs and beetle guts.

We have been called to manifest the contents of the Father's heart onto the Earth. There is no fear or defeat in the Father's heart, and so we should stop partnering with the spirit of fear.

Despite the reality that fear sells and gets ratings, we need to rail against that narrative, because the will of God will never be accomplished through believers whose confidence is not in the Lord.

Like Genesis 1, the Lord wants to release onto the Earth, the light of his living Word, through His covenant sons.

IF YOU CARE, SHARE

If God speaks His desires, then why do we speak our fears?

If what the Lord speaks causes the supernatural realm to become a visible manifestation within our realm, then shouldn't we be more careful when using our creative breath?

An important step in seeing your destiny become a reality is learning to give language to the dreams and desires of your heart. You should be proclaiming, "Let there be..." and those closest to you should be hearing and seeing the results of your declaration.

When the Lord called me into ministry, He told me to share the details of my call with those who were the closest to me. This was important for two reasons:

1. Communication for their sake

   It was only fair that my friends and family know how and why I was changing. They needed to understand that my steps were being redirected, and they needed to know how they could support me.

2. Communication for my sake

   I needed to be accountable for the word of the Lord, and the call of God on my life.

When God speaks to you regarding the dreams and desires of your heart, it's important to not let His promises die in isolation. Job 22:28

says, "You will also declare a thing, and it will be established for you; So light will shine on your ways." It's vital that we learn to give language to the dreams and desires of our heart. If we care, then it's extremely important that we have the courage to share. Declaring the word of the Lord creates an atmosphere for faith; it frames our steps and it solidifies a new reality within our souls.

SELF TALK

Sometimes I will declare my goals almost as if they were prophetic words, "Darren, you will work out today. It will be tough, but it's going to be great." My Grandpa used to say, "Bob, that's my first name. I only use it when I talk to myself, because you have to talk to someone decent every once in a while."

Communication is such an incredible gift from God. It's the way by which relationship is made possible. When there's a breakdown in communication, there's a breakdown in relationship.

Self-talk is important, but what do you do when you run out of words? You shift yourself from the natural to the supernatural, from a place of logic to speaking in our heavenly prayer language. Speaking in tongues, Paul says, is a way for the Holy Spirit to actually intercede through our spirit, therefore "building ourselves up" (1 Corinthians 14:4) in the Lord. Think about it. When you pray in tongues, you are literally embedding an encoded and heavenly message into the atmosphere and into your very DNA. We are going to see in just a moment that because of sin, the default pattern of our soul tends to have a negative bent. So, talk to yourself, sing over yourself, bless yourself, and speak in tongues.

SET THE COURSE

Harvey's wife had just discovered his problem with pornography. In her anger, she shouted, "If you don't love me, then let's just get divorced!" Rather than confessing his sin, repenting, and attempting to communicate his love for her, he shot back, "Fine!" Now her greatest concerns had just been confirmed; she now knew that he didn't actually love her. She felt abandoned by her husband because he wasn't able to properly communicate. This couple followed through with their divorce, despite neither party actually wanting it. Every day, marriages are blown to smithereens because someone, while angry, used the "D Word", and neither party were healthy enough to recognize the destructive power of their own words.

We frame our future with our words. We create choices and options by what we speak. We can paint the possibility of a future filled with faith, hope, and love, or we can create a future that is dismal and bleak.

Jesus never did any miracles without first making a declaration. He would speak, and then the miracle would manifest. Our breath is the instrument by which God creates. In Genesis 2:7 it says, "then the LORD God formed the man of dust from the ground and breathed into his nostrils the breath of life, and the man became a living creature." It's time for us to begin framing the future with the breath of life.

THE CHOICE *IS* THE PATTERN INTERRUPT

When we choose not to speak, our silence is louder than words. When we shut down because we are offended, our behavior is deafening.

Proverbs 18:19 says, "A brother offended is more unyielding than a strong city, and quarreling is like the bars of a castle."

When we become offended, we become fortified, or boarded up like a haunted house. There is no longer any receiving or giving. You are now stonewalled and shut down; incapable of possessing the ability to do what's necessary to work through the circumstance. Offense can become an addiction, a series of pattern loops that begin to define us. This pattern, like all patterns, becomes predictable. Ruled by offense, participants run from relationship to relationship, job to job, and church to church, constantly feeling rejected, shut down, and controlled. What many don't realize is, offense is a choice. When we carry offense, we are actually choosing to withhold forgiveness, thereby stepping out of a covenant of grace and back into an expired covenant of works. Underneath the covenant of works the broken relationship cannot be reconciled until a greater work dwarfs the sin. The offender must then begin tap dancing, performing, and proving themselves in order for the relationship to be made right again. This pattern is a common part of dysfunctional marriages and relationships. Peace within the relationship is contingent on works. As long as each participant performs as expected, then a sense of calm can be maintained. Such environments are breeding grounds for secret sin because transparency isn't valued; it's all about the show, and the show must go on.

PATTERN INTERRUPT FOR POOR COMMUNICATION

1. Put down the "Should Stick"

   When was the last time you beat someone with a "should stick"? A "should stick" is a statement that begins with, "You should..." Sometimes when we think we are being the most helpful, we are actually just verbalizing our negative judgments that really aren't that helpful.

2. Avoid Word Cursing

   A word curse is a negative, identity-framing statement, or expression, that reduces another's character because of an observed behavior. Think of it as a demonic prophetic word; a word released that predicts your inevitable failure in a specific area. A word curse is composed of universal statements that involve the use of words such as "always," "never," "again," "so," "every time," "such a," and "everyone." For example: "You always mess everything up." This particular statement has been framed through a judgment, so repentance is futile. Avoid generalized, negative judgments in your speech.

3. Put Down the Gun

   You wouldn't shoot your dog just because he was anemic; you would find out what the problem was. Sometimes addressing the issue directly doesn't seem satisfying enough; sometimes we feel that people deserve to be verbally punished. Getting mean/getting personal instead of addressing the issue is like shooting the dog instead of figuring out the real problem.

The choice *is* the pattern interrupt.

Instead of offense being your default response, you can make a choice to not shut down. As cliché as it sounds I would encourage you to ask yourself the question, "What would Jesus do?" In Ephesians 5, husbands are encouraged to love their wives like Christ loved the Church, by laying their lives down for them. When we are sinned against, it's important to remember that Jesus was also sinned against, and the way He dealt with the injustice was to satisfy it, with His love and His very life.

The pattern interrupt is the choice to forgive, because forgiveness obliterates offense. Once we have sabotaged the dysfunctional jargon that would typically frame a conversation, we can actually address the issues with a posture of undeserved kindness, rather than deserved punishment. In this kind of culture, positive change is unavoidable, because it's a culture of grace, and true grace is always transformational.

HOW TO BE A STONEWALL

3 Tips for Avoiding Confrontation

A stonewall is incapable of loving because it's composed of several inanimate objects. Stonewalls don't love and they don't respond, therefore they make for a lousy role model, but if for some reason you want to be like a stonewall, here are some tips.

1. Silent Stonewall

   Avoid conflict by remaining silent. A good stonewall doesn't respond. Refuse to participate in conversation.

2. Disconnected Stonewall

   Do your thing, focus on you, engage in your stuff and disappear within yourself. Stonewalls don't engage with others. Disconnect by disappearing. Fold your arms, and say things like, "Whatever," when confronted. If possible, don't speak, stonewalls don't speak (when tempted to respond refer back to rule #1).

3. The Disappearing Stonewall

   Again, see rule #1, and when things get really intense, weird or just too personal, simply disappear. This entails standing up and leaving the room when someone is grilling you.

WHAT'S YOUR NAME?

Each night when I'd lay Abigail in her crib I would tell her, "Abigail, your name means 'the father's joy' because, you bring me joy." Then I would kiss her on the head and say, "Goodnight." Still to this day, Abigail can tell you what her name means and why it is significant. Peter - my son - knows that his name means "rock", because he is solid and dependable. My daughter "Sophia" is at the age where I'm not asking her what her name means, I'm still telling her, it means "wisdom", and just in case you are wondering, my name means "Great", and no, I'm not making that up.

Biblically, a name communicates your reputation, power and authority. A name was so significant that several times in the Bible God actually changed people's name to signify their new identity.

Revelation 3:12-13 says, "I will make him a pillar in the temple of my God. Never shall he go out of it, and I will write on him the name of my God, and the name of the city of my God, the new Jerusalem, which comes down from my God out of heaven, and my own new name. He who has an ear, let him hear what the Spirit says to the churches."

In Christ, we get a new name, and a new identity. We are marked with the name of Christ, and therefore His power, reputation and authority become our own. When you are in Christ, you don't have to prove yourself, because He has already proven himself, and as you rest, the testimony of His finished work shines through you. In Christ, we don't have to strive to be us, nor do we have to fear that we are going to lose the edge that defines us.

You don't have to fear that you are going to lose yourself in the midst of all the noise. You have your Father's undivided attention, and until that's enough, He will probably keep you hidden. I know guys who claw and scream, like little baby eagles, trying to get noticed, trying to get some affirmation from people, and God protects them, by hiding them under His big eagle wings.

You are who He says you are.

You are a dream of God.

He has redeemed you, called you, and even named you.

It's time to reframe your present by writing the stories of the future, today; by singing tomorrow's worship songs, tonight; by declaring your new name "warrior", over yourself, even if you're still in the winepress, hiding, like a little baby. It has to start sometime. Why not now?

THE SPOKEN WORD

After forty days of fasting the serpent came to Jesus in the wilderness and began to tempt him. The enemy came at Him three times and with three scenarios. Jesus replied with the same weapon each and every time - with the Word of God. Ephesians 6:17 says that the Word of God is the sword of the Spirit; it is our only weapon against the enemy.

Jesus was locked and loaded with the Word of God was able to recall just the right word that would serve as a specialized weapon for each and every individualized attack. Each time Jesus quoted a scripture from memory, His breath would give birth to a literal sound wave that could be used to literally render temptation useless. Sound waves can be a powerful weapon in the spirit as they are actually composed of air pressure, that travels through light. It wasn't enough for Jesus to simply know the word; He had to speak the word in order to weaponize the word. Never underestimate the supernatural power of the spoken word of God. If it has the power to redeem and restore communities, cities, regions and nations, then it can most certainly transform us to the very core of who we are.

USE YOUR SWORD

1. Meditate

    Forget sword drills. Reading the word is not a competition. There may be a place for speed-reading the Word of God, but not unless you have a separate time when you can meditate on God's Word. Meditating involves taking your time and reflecting on each word of each line. Receiving it slowly as if eating a good steak.

2. Step in

    The Word of God is a gateway. Don't just read the text, step into it, and experience it.

3. Study

    When engaging with a text, feel free to take some time to study the text. Dive into a commentary or study Bible. Read about the history of the text, the scenarios and situations that inspired the text. Find the similarities between the author's day and our own.

4. Pray

Pray (or sing) the text over yourself. Some scriptures are easier than others. There isn't a formula for this. It's all about partnering with the Holy Spirit to find a way to declare God's Word over yourself. In a way, it's kind of like clothing yourself in God's Word.

THE KEY THAT WORKS

In 2016, Patricia King had a vision in which she was moving up a golden escalator to a new level in the spirit. The Lord brought her to a door called "Revival" but it was locked and guarded by an angel. Patricia tried a key called "Hope" but the key didn't work. She then tried another key called "Desperation," but the angel would still not permit her to enter. She tried yet again, a third key, this one was called "Expectation." The angel told her that she was very close, but it didn't possess the ability to unlock the door. The final key worked, it unlocked the door, it was the key of "Faith-Filled Prayers."

Do you want access to the room that possesses the light of God, the glory of God, the beauty of God, and holy fire of God? Then you need the key that works. Desperation is marketable and expectation is fun, but faith-filled prayers open the door of revival where literally anything becomes possible.

The key is your voice, your declaration, your knowing that God is going to show up because of you. We have to begin speaking the substance of Heaven into the Earth and declaring the desires of God. See Jesus, the pattern prophet, He simply spoke what His father was carrying in His heart. Your breath is more than a vibration, its frequency, clothed in light. Atmospheres are created, darkness expelled, miracles manifested, demons rebuked, all through faith-filled declarations.

SNAP - "OUCH!" - OUT OF IT

According to psycologytoday.com it's estimated that 70% to 80% of our thoughts - approximately 40,000 thoughts per day - are negative. This would explain why there is so much fear-based, negative speech within the Church. The average person lives in a subconscious pool of doubt.

But what if you could literally snap out of it? Check out the rubber band, "snap out of it" strategy. Despite my research, I believe that it's fair to say that nobody really knows who's behind this strategy (although there are several PHD's and one church that claim authorship).

The concept is simple: Place a rubber band around your wrist, and whenever you think a negative thought, snap it. If necessary, snap up to three times per negative thought. The physical pain will get you out of your head, and back into the real world, and psychologist say it's clinically proven to work.

From what I've been told, shooting rubber bands at negative people doesn't have the same effect, but I hope to conduct my own experiment to see for myself. Keep posted for test results.

SPEAK THE FUTURE YOU WOULD LIKE TO LIVE IN

If battles are won, diseases healed, demons rebuked, and atmospheres created by our words and word choice, then wouldn't it be wise for us to be strategic in how we speak?

Don't preach your peeves or preferences; preach the good news of the gospel. Don't project the issues of your soul into an atmosphere. Subvert the militant spirit of negativity with the spirit of thanksgiving and joy. Let us use our creative breath to pull the justice and restoration of God that's typically associated with the future into the present, and let's create the kind of world we would be proud to live in.

HOW TO BRING HEAVEN TO EARTH AT WORK

1. Gather other believers to stand as priests. Unity brings a commanded blessing.

2. Gather for Bible Study or Studies, prayer groups, etc.

3. Discern what spirits are wreaking havoc within the environment.

4. Identify open doors (people, places, circumstances that may have given the enemy a legal right for the enemy).

5. Repent for open doors and partnering with the demonic.

6. Ask for the Lord's judgments and justice.

7. Begin to displace the chaos with prayer.

8. Ask the Lord's strategies in establishing a new and Heavenly culture.

USE WATER ON FIRE

Right when you're about to be triggered, rather than getting all worked up and fighting fire with fire, allow the presence of the Lord to be your pattern interrupt. For far too long we've been fighting darkness with darkness, and striving with striving, but I think that the Lord wants us to begin winning some battles by engaging with the opposite spirit. Instead of getting all hot and bothered, we can choose to lay down beside green pastures and even rest while the Lord releases water upon the fire. In the Old Testament, we see that God likes to win battles on behalf of His people, and He also likes to prepare for us banqueting tables in the presence of our enemies.

The Crusades and the 1980's taught us that aggressive and churchy militancy just ends up looking weird and certainly won't redeem the culture. What America needs is not another *March for Jesus.*

We can't obtain influence by demanding it or even declaring it. We will have to partner with the spirit of Christ Jesus, and like Jesus, we will have to love the world enough to serve her, and lay our lives down for her.

For God so loved the world that He sent you and I - His sons and daughters - to be the body of Christ; to demonstrate the power of Christ; to herald the hope of Christ, and to point people to salvation, made possible through Christ.

Like Christ, with our words, we can reveal what's in the Father's heart. With our declarations we can create realms that are infused with faith, hope, and love. With our actions we can demonstrate what the Father's love actually looks like. With our surrender we can reveal the faithfulness of God. With our worship we can reveal the very character and nature of God. With our love we can reveal the Father's heart for justice and mercy. With our devotion we can reveal the kind of passion that cannot be quenched by death. Through our faith, we can demonstrate the reality of the Kingdom of Heaven on the face of the Earth.

Many are hoping to get back to a kind of Christianity that hasn't been seen since the first century. However, there is a form of Christianity that simply hasn't yet been seen on the Earth.

The Lord is about to take us back to the future, where no man has ever gone before.

3 DIRECTIVES:

1. Commit yourself to the art of communication

2. Choose to not allow lack to frame your words

3. Begin to share the dreams of desires of your heart.

SMALL GROUP DISCUSSION QUESTIONS:

- How have you seen the power of words demonstrated within your life?

- Have you tried the key of "Faith Filled Prayers"?

- Where has God called you to intentionally create atmospheres where He can show up and show off?

ACTIVATION PRAYER:

Thank you Lord that you have given me ears to hear, and eyes to see. Thank you that you are leading and guiding me in this unique time in human history. Teach me how to pray. Teach me how to stand. Retrain my tongue so that I only speak what I first hear you say.

Thank you that you are releasing to me the courage to walk by faith and not by sight. Thank you for giving me the shield of faith by which I can extinguish all the fiery darts of the enemy.

I hear you inviting me, to rebuke the storms, to get out of the boat, to heal the sick, raise the dead, and cast out demons, make disciples of nations, and to give my life for the cause of the gospel.

Let me never be ashamed of the gospel.

In Jesus name amen.

10
GREEN LIGHT

Now Go!

"He said to them, 'Go into all the world and preach the gospel to all creation.'"

- Mark 16:15

CHUCK

Personally, as a young minister, I loved Ephesians 4. It gave me permission to label people according to their gifting or personality. Fivefold ministry empowered me to think of ministry like a video store with five different rows of movies, all separated by genre.

I fit in the pastoral category. I was a pastor-in-a-box. This was liberating because it meant that I didn't have to be an evangelist. My job was to love people, and let the evangelists get people saved. The problem was, after two years in ministry and never leading anyone to the Lord outside the church, I got really frustrated.

"God," I cried out, "I want to see the power of the Gospel."

Greg Daley, our church's on-staff evangelist, always had all these fresh stories of leading people to the Lord. I wanted stories. I wanted to see if I could do "the stuff." One day I asked Greg to take me out into the field and show me the ropes. We saw people saved, healed and delivered, and we were only out for an hour.

I wanted to see if I had the goods. The next day I went out by myself. I drove to a part of town that was known for drug problems and systemic poverty. As I parked my car, I saw an older guy sitting out in his backyard, rocking back and forth in his wooden patio rocking chair. I locked my car, and then double-locked my car. Two sets of beeps, just to let people know that my car was locked and perhaps had an alarm, which it didn't. I swallowed the lump in the back of my throat and then, like Greg Daley, I walked right up to the guy with a serious Batman-like face. It was on. I asked him how he was doing. He responded with a sarcastic joke while staring forward at an apartment across the street. He was watching something. I asked him if I could sit down at his patio table, and after assuring him that I wasn't selling anything, he invited me to hang out. He explained to me that these particular neighbors were running a brothel. The mom was actually pimping out her own daughters. He would sit there in his backyard and watch these men come and go throughout the day, in complete disgust.

I told him my name, and he told me that his was Chuck. I disclosed that I was a pastor to which he responded with, "I've never been visited by a pastor before." Chuck told me about his upbringing, about his mom who had a habit of bringing home a variety of men, about the beatings he received from them, and about the night his mom took him deep into the city, down a dark alley, and abandoned him because she didn't feel fit to be his mother any longer. He told me about the war, and about his regrets. Chuck was at the end of his life, and he didn't want to feel guilty anymore.

I asked Chuck, if he died today, if he knew if he would go to Heaven. He knew for certain that he wouldn't. I asked him if he would like to have his sins washed away and receive forgiveness from Jesus, and he said "yes".

When I got to the part of the prayer where you say, "Forgive me of all my sins," Chuck deterred from the script and responded, "But I've done so many." At this point he began to cry, and after being so moved by his humility, I joined him. Holding Chuck's hand, I struggled to finish the prayer.

When we were done praying, I taught him how to pray for himself. I would return in the following weeks with a Bible and different books. He never felt comfortable going to church despite my offer to pick him up. Chuck's life was changed, and so was mine. I was no longer a pastor-in-box. I was a bonafide evangelist, just like Pastor Greg.

I quickly learned that the only thing that can really limit me is what I call myself. I don't want to dis titles, job descriptions, and Ephesians 4, but I have learned that the title of "son" dwarfs all other titles.

So yes, I'm a pastor, but I don't really see myself as a pastor. I really actually see myself as more of a superhero. My job is to inspire, save the day, and make things right in the world. My job is to inspire you to do the same.

Someday

"Someday," is what a dreamer tells himself while watching Seinfeld marathons in the middle of the day. Everybody has a dream, and yet many dismiss the hope of a glorious future because of what appears to be the lack of momentum.

"Today," is what an athlete says when they wake up at 3 AM to begin training for a marathon.

Are you a someday person or a today person?

Do these phrases look familiar?

"Someday I will lose that weight."

"Someday I will clean that garage."

"Someday I will quit using."

"Someday I will flush that toilet."

"Someday I will discipline that kid."

"Someday I will tell my wife I love her."

"Someday" implies that the universe will magically supply the pixie dust needed to eventually succeed, and when that time never comes, sometimes, we blame the discouragement on warfare and the lack of progress on the devil. Don't believe the New Age mumbo-jumbo; intent will not land you a prosperous destiny any more than staring at a toilet will catch you a fish. James 2:17 says that faith without works is dead. Don't wait and see. Time isn't something you want to put your faith in. If it's not worth doing today, is it really something that's worth putting off for someday? Don't tease yourself. Yes, God is sovereign, but He's not going to reward those who are not stewarding the time that they have been given. Time is ticking away. You aren't waiting on God; He's waiting on you. Turn off the TV.

The truth is you're not going to win the lottery in the future; you won it two thousand years ago. Stop waiting for something you already possess. Paul says it best in 2 Corinthians 6:1, "Behold, *now* is the favorable time; behold, *now* is the day of salvation."

It's go time.

For generations the Israelites had waited, and waited, and waited. Jesus ended that wait. The day of salvation was upon the Corinthian church and they didn't see it. Most of us are in the same boat; waiting for God to come and save humanity, meanwhile Paul is like, "Yo, it's done. Now get to work."

You are living in the era of God's mercy and grace. The door to the ark is still open, and you are waaaaaaaiting for what now?!

Tim Keller - my favorite Presbyterian from New York City - once gave an extraordinary analogy. He said:

If a King goes to battle and his armies are defeated, upon hearing the news he will gather his strategists into his war room and begin planning for the next battle; but if that King is victorious in battle, he won't gather his strategists upon hearing the news, he will gather his heralds, and he will send them out to begin declaring the good news.

Keller continued to explain that Christianity differed from every other religion in that we are not trying to figure out how to win a battle. The battle has been won. Jesus defeated Satan, death, hell, and the grave. The King is victorious, and He is sending out newsboys to proclaim the good news; the gospel.

Does your theology frame a victorious King leading a winning team, or do you believe that everything is on the verge of total annihilation? Does your proclamation of the gospel reflect the good news of the cross, or is it full of angst, militant rhetoric, and involve bunkers, canned goods and automatic weapons?

So make a commitment to lose all your religious jargon that would base your lack of movement on God's will. Unless you're a literal slug, don't blame your slow pace on God.

Truth is your pattern interrupt. Stop being hyper-spiritual and take responsibility. You got a green light so put your foot on that gas pedal and move.

PATTERN INTERRUPT FOR THE SPIRIT OF LETHARGY

Some spirits can't be cast out. Here's what to do to break out of the realm of apathy and sluggish behavior.

1. Begin Sleeping

    Sleep is good for your spirit, soul, and body. If you love yourself, start taking care of yourself. Eight hours of sleep each night will improve your memory, add years to your life, curb inflammation (reducing risk of heart disease, stroke, diabetes, arthritis, and premature aging), fuel creativity, significantly boost your energy levels, help you be aware of the details, boost metabolism, lower stress, and help one overcome depression.

2. Cold Shower

I take a freezing cold shower in the mornings because it wakes me up and snaps me out of sleepy time mode. Cold showers also have numerous health benefits including: enhanced immunity (to fight off infection and even cancer); boosts glands including thyroid, adrenals, ovaries/testes, improving hormonal activity; boost metabolism (fighting off type 2 diabetes, obesity, gout, rheumatic diseases, and depression); normalizes blood pressure; decreases chronic pain; good for the skin; improves kidney function; improves hemorrhoids and varicose veins; helps with insomnia.

Tips for Beginners:

Take a shower at regular temperature and soap up. Use your last three minutes to rinse and shiver. Set a clock or timer near your shower. Your tolerance level will eventually change and you may even get to the point where you enjoy a cold shower the whole time.

3. Exercise

You don't need a gym membership. Go to YouTube and find a 20-30 minute routine. Commit to sweat 10 minutes a day. If you go the whole 20-30 minutes, God bless you.

- Tips for Beginners: Be accountable. Post your goals on your favorite social media platform. Ask people to ask you how you are doing. One thing I do, I have workout equipment everywhere; dumbbells in my home office, a swiss ball in my bathroom, and a pull up bar in my closet. It works, I see it and I go for it. I can always spare five minutes to fit in 100 sit-ups, etc.

4. Diet

Diet is more important than exercise. Food is fuel. If you eat bad food you're going to feel bad. If you eat great food, you're going to feel great. You can see my diet plan and supplements on my website at www.isupernaturalist.com and checkout my "now" page.

5. Grow Spiritually

Find a church, go to it every weekend, connect with a mid-week group and schedule a meeting with a pastor. Your spiritual nutrition is just as important as your physical nutrition. They supplement each other and are inextricably linked. Develop a spiritual growth plan with your pastor and get plugged in.

6. Full Time

Sometimes when we have too much freedom in our schedule we discover that we actually have no freedom in our schedule. Stop diversifying, and go full time. Become a full time student, a full time employee, or a full time volunteer. Research shows people who work are healthier than those who don't.

TODAY

In Psalm 118:24, David had this amazing revelation, "Today is the day that the Lord has made, we will rejoice and be glad in it." God created today as a special gift for you, because He loves you. He breathed today into existence, so that He could be glorified through your satisfaction. Like David, our response should be to rejoice; be joyful, and find gladness within this gift of life.

This Psalm is filled with the kind of joy that accompanies expectancy. Every morning should be filled with exuberant suspense; His mercies are new every morning and each day is a day loaded with hidden potential. God surrounds us each and every day with supernatural opportunities, but we have to have the eyes to see and the faith to engage.

Many of us need some new supernatural gear. Perhaps you need a new expectation generator, a faith thermostat, a hope dispenser, or a doubt extinguisher. Sadly, these things can't be found at Wal-Mart.

So, it's all about today...

Today is the day of salvation.

Today is the day you go for a jog.

Today is the day to receive your miracle.

Today is the day to look for a new job.

Today is the day to start a diet.

Today is the day you go out for coffee with a friend.

It has to start sometime, why not today?

GO

In the scriptures, every encounter with God always proceeds with a sending off, a *bon voyage*. If God ever meets with you face-to-face, you bet it's going to proceed with a two-letter word, "go."

God met with Abraham, revealed his future to him, and then kicked him out of Ur with one word "go." Then there was Isaiah's crazy visionary encounter. God forgave him of his sins, cleansed his lips with burning coal, made him a prophet and then told him to, "go." Then there was Jesus. He recruited his disciples; signed them up for the fast track for to leadership, and then He died. The good news is, He resurrected, and just before floating off the planet, He looked His disciples in the eyes, squinted, and said, "Guys," squinting his eyes even tighter He continued with a whisper, "It's go time," and just like that His feet begin to lift off the ground. He flexed his core muscles to keep His balance, and looked up as if gazing into the eyes of His Father. He then lifted his right index finger, pointing up at the cloud he would pass through while keeping the other fist clenched tight. The true and perfect Superman had saved the day! Then all of sudden, like a rocket, He broke the sound barrier and disappeared into the realm of Heaven. Jesus had to move on to the next part of his mission, which meant He had to *go*.

Go doesn't mean, "Get busy."

Go is a commandment; a mandate to begin engaging with the mission of God. It's an invitation to begin taking immediate action in carrying out the Father's business on the Earth.

You and I have been invited to join His mission. It's not just an evangelistic commission, it's a Kingdom commission. We've been given the green light to get started in the "greater things" that Jesus talked about - to represent His kingly rule and reign, and to establish His government of peace.

"Go," communicates movement, and movement requires a change of focus. It shifts our focus from ourselves to others, from the past onto the future, from the fear of people's preferences to the awe of His presence.

The great commission doesn't require your perfection, just your submission. In order to be truly obedient we have to entrust that Jesus is capable of using us despite us. Sometimes our greatest healing comes as a result of ministering to others. "Go," won't allow you to get self-obsessed and lost in all consuming self-healing efforts. "Don't go," will always embellish all your imperfections so that you stay. "Don't go," will exploit the "facts" against you so that you remove yourself from the field before you ever got to even play in the game. You don't get the privilege to disqualify yourself from ministry, because you were never qualified to begin with.

There's only one appropriate response to, "go," and it's, "Sure thing, whatever you say!"

COMMITMENT

Timothy Keller, once said, "Reason can get you to probability, but only commitment can get you to certainty."

No commitment, no responsibility. No responsibility, no authority.

If you want an upgrade in authority, then you may need an upgrade in your commitments. Many of us lack commitment; and some of us even have little to no commitment in our commitments. Life has a way of turning into a hodgepodge of detached obligations. We joylessly perform in marriage, work, and church life, and we find that our faith is as limp as a washrag.

The supernatural power of God and commitment is interconnected. Heaven doesn't compartmentalize things like we do. No commitment, no power. Powerlessness doesn't mean that power doesn't exist; it just means you don't have any. For example, electrical power can be turned on and off; likewise, Heaven's voltage can be turned off like a faucet within your life. If you're thinking you'd like to get your power back on, you may want to jumpstart your personal revival by assessing your commitments and investments, or lack thereof.

Drilling for oil requires a commitment. You find a spot, and you start drilling. Before you find the black gold, you have to get through the dirt, the hard rock, and then a lot of spitting mud. It's really messy and a lot of hard work. Many people quit. Some throw in the towel when they were just inches away from a breakthrough. The mud gets flying, everything starts getting dirty, and people start shutting everything down. The messier life gets, the closer you are to striking oil. If you only knew all times you quit just before striking oil you'd kick your own butt. You don't get oil without a commitment, a big drill, patience, and an ocean of mud. Success is *always* messy.

When my son, Peter, was two-year-old and he'd get afraid, he'd shiver and say, "*Scaa-aaaa-aared.*" I left the commitment talk for the end of the book on purpose. I didn't want for you to get *scaaaaaaared.* If I had mentioned it in the introduction you would have word-cursed me, closed the book and put it on your shelf next to your dusty copy of Wayne Grudem's *Systematic Theology;* that is, assuming you read introductions.

Perhaps you tried committing to a church, revivalist, or an MLM, and ended up drinking the Kool-Aid, laundering funds to the Caymans, and selling purified-dehydrated-water to your friends and family [just add water]. Perhaps the fire of commitment has burned you, and now you're a spiritual nomad who jumps around the country, attending supernatural schools in hotel conference rooms. Now I am all for a good school at the Days Inn or cruise ship conference, but don't try to find intimacy from a one-night-stand. If you don't have Christ loving friends who know the real, imperfect you, avoid the hysteria of supernatural manifestations, and seek first a community of real people who will love you no matter what. Don't seek supernatural phenomenon in order to fill a void. Seek first the Kingdom of God and His righteousness and all these things will be added unto you. Being supernatural doesn't mean you have to be weird. You can be real, normal, healthy, and God can just so happen to do crazy cool stuff through you.

Powerful commitments are those that build on a healthy foundation of mutual love. If you are manipulated into a commitment, your loyalty will only be held intact by fear, shame, and control. If you build on love, your choice to commit will reflect the fruit of the spirit. Loving God and others is the great commandment, and upon that commandment everything else is hinged. We are treading in some deep water right now.

Now is the time! Not someday. TODAY!

It's time to confront those emotions, memories, and shadows of the past; lasso them like a cowboy; wrestle them down like Ken Shamrock, and demand that they surrender to the Lordship of Jesus Christ. Make a choice to forgive, and release those who have taken advantage of your freedom to commit. Forgive them and entrust them into the arms of Jesus.

You Were Born For This Day

Out of one hundred billion galaxies

Existing in one hundred billion star systems

Out of seven billion people

You have your own genetic makeup

Your thumbprint is yours alone

You can create art

You can write a song

You are depended upon by others who love you

You are enormously significant

- Unknown

My friend, Jamie Dickson once said, "This generation was born for this time." I know this, I believe this, I have taught this. It's even somewhat of a mantra for me, and yet the way he said it, it was different, and it caught my attention. Despite how awkward you may feel at times, there has never been a moment in history that is as right for you as right now. You were born for this time! Another era wouldn't have worked for you, it had to be now.

Do you ever feel overwhelmed with a sense of insignificance? Wondering if your contribution has any benefit at all? Submitting to insecurity is like allowing water to be poured on the fire of your soul. Entertaining demeaning thoughts about yourself is not humility; it's pride, and it's a sin. What good am I in this world and to the Kingdom of Heaven if I believe myself to be worthless and void of anything good?

Psalm 139

God knows you intimately. When you get out of bed, and when you are driving to work, He knows every fleeting thought that is being squeezed through your morning brain. He knows your habits, and the triggers to your addictions. He finishes your sentences before your tongue forms the first word. His hand is upon you, and if you only knew how involved He is in the details of your life, the joy of such knowledge would overwhelm your earthly ability to function. We can run, but we can't hide. His presence is everywhere. In the midst of angels, joy, and glory; to the sunken depths of depravity and darkness – He is present.

He created your inmost being, you've been knit together in your mother's womb. Your frame was not hidden from Him when you were made in the secret place. How precious are His thoughts towards you? How vast is the sum of them? If you could count them, they would outnumber the sands of grains of sand.

He knows you. He knows your heart. He knows your thoughts. He knows your offensive ways, and yet He loves you, and will lead you in the way everlasting.

GOD BE WITH ME, SHOW ME THE ENEMY

This the part of the show where Morpheus takes you to the Matrix arsenal. Myriads of stocked shelves go scrolling by you like pages on a search engine. This is the moment when you realize that everything you have ever needed to be successful has been available to you all along. Every tool, resource, and relationship has been right here, like unopened Christmas gifts, with your name on them. There is no lack of resources in Heaven.

Romans 8:31-32 states, "What then shall we say to these things? If God is for us, who can be against us? He who did not spare his own Son but gave him up for us all, how will he not also with him graciously give us all things?"

Your training has been for this moment. The curtains have been pulled. You can't see because you are being blinded by Heaven's spotlight. It's shining on you, because it's your time to shine.

God is for you, so why are you fighting yourself? Since the day you were born Hell as thrown you curve balls, trying to strike you out, bum you out, and get you to quit. In this race, as long as you don't quit, you win. The question at this moment is, are you running your race?

What if God the Father could tuck you into bed tonight, what do you think He'd say? He would probably tell you what He sees in you, and how much He loves you. He would probably make a promise to never leave you nor forsake you. He'd probably tell you, that with Him, all things are possible. So why not let him tuck you into bed tonight, and before he turns out the lights, why not give to Him your all of your fears.

Remember, it's not the spoon that needs to bend; it's your mind. The thing that is keeping you from third world miracles is right between your ears. Most modern Christians have received more Christian training in the first year of their walk with God than two thirds of the world. You might not think that you know your Bible, but chances are, you know too much. We've been trained to be trainers, who will need training, so that the trainers who are training trainers, can be trained. Bottom line, you've probably received enough training. At a certain point, you need to allow God to fill you to such a point that you begin overflowing. Let the love of God spill into you, over you, and out of you. Be ye therefore filled even now!!

The Holy Spirit can do in an hour through a surrendered soul what it would take an entire organization to do in ten years. In Acts 2, five thousand men are saved in a day; from 1904-1905 over one hundred thousand decisions were made for Christ in the country of Wales, through the collaboration of the Holy Spirit and a twenty-six-year old named Evan Roberts.

We haven't seen anything yet. History hasn't seen anything yet. Our greatest dreams don't have the capability of grasping the greatness of God's dreams for this world, and you have a part to play.

God is with you, in you, and upon you. Pull up your bootstraps because it has begun.

QUIT

Kris Vallotton has this amazing sermon called *Follow Your Favor.* The premise is that we need to examine the areas of our life that God is blessing, and pursue them. Perhaps God told you to get on a horse sixty years ago, and now you are beating the horse because he's not moving. Sure, maybe God never told you to get off the horse, but perhaps God thought you had enough common sense to know that the average lifespan of a horse is twenty-five to thirty years. You're frustrated because he's not moving, but that's because he's dead. It's not time for a resurrection; it's time for a much-deserved funeral. Get off your dead horse!

Many people quit before they come into a significant breakthrough. This is because they lack vision, strategy, and perseverance. However, there are just as many people who don't have vision, strategy, and perseverance, and they never quit, start, or breakthrough into anything. There's too many people riding dead horses and think they are going somewhere; life is way too short to be following blind cowboys. We need to see where we are at and where we are going. Once you get a vision for the future, quit your past, and let go of everything that is dead.

I once met with this couple that was quitting our church; I didn't want them to leave, and the dude said to me, "When we moved here, we didn't know anybody. We came to this church and didn't know anyone. Now we have lots of friends here. We are going to a new church where we don't know anybody, and that's okay, because we will soon have lots of new friends there." The dude was so comfortable with change, and I sort of admired that. He and his family quit my church; it's what was best for their family. Skip a beat. Maybe you need to quit some stuff. Follow Christ and don't apologize for trying to be obedient to His leading.

HOW TO QUIT

1. Quit the right thing

   Most people don't know what to quit. They quit all the right things, and keep doing all the wrong things. Many quit stuff in order to feel less overwhelmed, only to find that they are just as overwhelmed with an empty whiteboard than they were with the full whiteboard. I've never heard anybody say, "I'm quitting potato chips, and Facebook, because I am just so stressed out." No, they quit their church's community group, go home, open a bag of potato chips, and stalk people on Facebook.

   Don't run from tension. The tension is good, and is always present just before significant change. Mediocrity hates change, and will do everything possible to rail against change catalysts.

2. Don't Fear Conflict

   Conflict is not a sign that you missed God. Avoiding conflict might be the thing that's holding you back from your favor. Many Christians would rather remain in a wilderness of passivity, than address some issues and move into a promised land of inheritance. Most couples get married and experience their first fight within twenty-four hours of marriage; if there's not maturity, the conflict may leave one of the partners saying, "I knew God didn't want me to marry this person," but in the Old Testament, God always used conflict as an opportunity to create intimacy between the Israelites and Himself. A relationship without conflict is no relationship at all. In times of conflict, we learn who we really are.

3. Be Assertive

Email is only good for setting up appointments and canceling your HBO subscription after the first free month. If you're going to quit something, be assertive, truthful and do it face-to-face, or worst case scenario, on the phone. Don't hide behind your technology. When we let our text messages do the talking, it costs us relational equity. A misunderstanding over email may take weeks to sort out; that same fight could have been resolved in less than an hour. When a fierce conversation is initiated by Facebook, email, or text, immediately pick-up your phone and schedule a face-to-face. If they won't meet you, there's nothing you can do but forgive, and wipe the dust off your feet.

As Christians, we must have the courage to engage in honoring, truthful and assertive conversations.

4. Hear from God

Hearing God's voice is so important in making significant decisions because it becomes an anchor point; a moment in time that we can go back to and remember what God said to do.

ENGAGE IN THE NEW

Once you jump off your dead horse, jump onto a new horse. Don't dillydally around the barn talking water-cooler smack with the old bitter cowboys; there's work to be done! Now's the time to engage, no excuses. You're not at the end of your story, you've just gotten past the introduction, and your autobiography is just about to begin.

And let's chat about your age. You – are – not – old! In light of eternity, you are a toddler. Some of the most apostolic lethal weapons in the Kingdom are in rest homes; they are pastoring, prophesying, evangelizing, teaching, and making an eternal impact. Your spirit will never get old, the Holy Spirit will never get old, and so why should the age of your physical body disqualify you from extraordinary supernatural wonders? It's time to engage.

To engage means that you are going to become personally invested within His Kingdom agenda as it is playing out here and now. To engage means that you are going to break up with Mr. Bitterness, and let him know that you are returning back to Mr. Forgiveness. It means, no more hanging out with the Pharisees and Sadducees - the haters and cynics. It means finding some fishers of men who are following Jesus, and engaging in the work of the Holy Spirit. To engage means that you are going to actively begin creating a 'Take Initiative Culture.'

CREATING A 'TAKE INITIATIVE' CULTURE

Car maintenance never calls for celebration. No one throws an oil changing party every three thousand miles, except for maybe Oil Can

Henry. You were all excited when you got that new car right? But now you have to wash it, put gas in it, change the oil, and get tune ups. No one ever said that owning a car was going to be so much work, but, if you love your car, you choose to take care of it.

Physical health, spiritual health, and romantic health are areas of big concern for most modern people. The problem is, there's no smartphone app that can make you healthy. You have to be your own catalyst for growth and health, lest you be your own worst enemy. Being healthy, growing in the Lord, and capturing the heart of your spouse is contingent on *you* taking initiative and engaging in these areas.

Jesus said to love others as you love yourself. Paul says for husbands to love their wives as they love their own bodies, by making her holy, cleansing her by the washing with water through the word, and presenting her as a radiant, without stain or wrinkle or any other blemish, but holy and blameless. So much gets lost in translation, because how many men actually love their body?

The problem is taking initiative means taking risk; it means that we are willing to fall down, fail, and get back up again for another round. My fear is that so many times we reward lukewarm behavior in the name of fairness.

A take initiative culture says we are going to reward the bold, the brave, and the fearless – because what greater sign of humility is there than to dare to share your opinion; to surrender your ideas for scrutiny, constructive criticism, and amazing questions.

There are many leaders who are afraid to formulate their own values, systems, and behaviors. There are amazing people who are scared to death to even share their own desires with their family and friends. As believers, sometimes we are trained into a lukewarm lifestyle of false humility therefore adopting defeater beliefs as truths. Here are a few lukewarm defeater beliefs that may be robbing you of being a great leader...

LUKEWARM DEFEATER BELIEFS:

- I'll just sit low in the boat.

- I'm not going to share how I feel, because last time I shared my feelings weren't validated.

- I can't volunteer or be involved because I don't have time.

- I don't know anything.

- I can't be vulnerable because people will see the real me, and reject me.

- I am weak.

THE TRUTH

If you stay silent, you're robbing people of a blessing. Fear tricks us into thinking that our silence keeps up safe. Courage says, "Get out of the darn boat!" Speak up; there's gold in your heart that could really help a lot of people.

Refuse to live in the darkness of silence. Share what's on your mind and what you are carrying in your heart.

You do have the time to engage with your destiny. You have as much time as everybody else. Choose to steward your time in the same way that you steward your finances.

Continue to grow. Try new things. Meet new people. Worship God with your passion and talents.

You are growing in wisdom, understanding, and discernment. You are reading the Bible, good books and articles. You are having quality conversations, and listening to your teacher, the Holy Spirit.

You can be vulnerable because you are infinitely accepted by your Heavenly Father.

You are strong. You can do all things through Christ who strengthens you.

A lukewarm life is not a conservative life, it is a faithless, godless, and boring life. Nobody wants to follow a wallflower. This world is looking for Christ-men and Christ-women who will dare to say, "Come, and follow me as I follow Christ."

Make a decision *today* to lead yourself out of passivity. Be the first to volunteer, to speak up, to lay hands on the sick, to greet a stranger with a smile and prophetic word. Be first to speak up, "Lord, if it be thou, bid me come unto thee on the water."

THE EXTRAORDINARY SWITCH

Despite what Oprah has told you, you can't make yourself remarkable. You, by nature, are not a good fixer upper. All the effort and money in the world is not going to be enough to repair what sin has demolished, but when you invited Jesus to come and reside within you. At that moment you became extraordinary; Heaven moved into you!

You are a dwelling place for the most-high God. His glory inhabits you; you are seated in glory. You have been raptured into the fudgy marshmallow realm of His honey glory. The old you has been whacked, R.I.P. Jesus flipped your switch from ordinary to extraordinary. You've been flipped on! It's time for your spirit to tell your soul what's up. It's time for your feelings to submit to the actuality of the cross. It's time to take a bath in the water of the Word and get clean of those germy defeater beliefs. All it takes is just a good scrubbing.

The extraordinary you need is oxygen. We get suffocated by so many things; negative Nancys, perfectionism, religion, self-righteousness, pride, arrogance, sin, etc., etc., etc. It's time to purge the dirge.

HOW TO PURGE THE DIRGE

1. Read your Bible! The Bible is full of glory, and it will mess you up.

2. Click 'hide' on all your negative Facebook friends; it will hide them from your news feed without them feeling rejected.

3. Quit watching so much cable news and find a new favorite channel, like Nickelodeon or the Food Network.

4. Find a new barber who doesn't grumble, gossip, and complain.

5. Find a new radio station; I would recommend oldies – there's a lotta glory on the Beetles.

6. Quit reading books on the end times – it's not the end, it's only the beginning. Your Starbucks app is not the mark of the beast.

7. Go to Nordstrom. Seek style advice, try on new clothes, but don't buy them. Find a thrift store in a yuppie part of town and buy the same clothes there. Throw away some of your old clothes. New threads communicate that God is doing a new thing in you.

8. Quit smoking. The new extraordinary you doesn't need to be smelling all funky and musty. Cigarettes will eventually kill you, which means that they are part of the devil's strategy to steal, kill, and destroy you. Disengage with this means of seeking counterfeit shalom. Get your house, car, and clothes professionally cleaned, and remind yourself that the water of the Word has washed you. Anoint yourself with perfumed oil, and let the fragrance of Heaven restore healing and health.

SO WHAT'S THE LORD DOING?

1. Detox: The Church is getting clean of religious performance.

2. Drown: We are sinking into a new depth within His heart; the love of Christ shifting the way we see the world.

3. Drive: We are hightailing it into Canaan. The wilderness was overrated.

Fear-based reactions will no longer jive with the Church of Jesus Christ. He is giving us eyes to see so that we can connect supernatural solutions with Earth's injustices. Hopelessness is being eradicated through our faith-filled words and actions. The demonic realm is losing its foothold in your region. Deliverance is becoming commonplace.

Popularity may come with the turf, as people want to be with people who are connected. You won't have to be flashy; a white suit won't be necessary. Your speech won't have to be eloquent, but spell check will still be essential.

They will seek you out like zombies after the living. They will smell the freedom on you from miles away. They will demand truth, and you will give them Jesus; those who believe will find their prison doors easily opened.

God will speak to you in dreams. Visions will be normal. You won't doubt. You won't fear.

Where you go, revolution will follow. The ground will shake, creation will groan, and your spirit will confirm, "It really was the time."

Now is your time, the minute, and the moment; the spirit of revival is in the air. From the ashes, mud, and mire is coming a forgotten generation; the sons and daughters of God are about to be revealed.

THE PRODIGALS ARE COMING HOME

I love the picture of the prodigal son's father standing out on the road, looking into the distance, waiting for the day that his lost son returns home. I can see God the Father standing out on the road, as an army of innumerable lost sons and daughters begin to emerge on the horizon. I can see the Father picking up His robes and awkwardly running. I can see His tears bailing from His eyes like water off a flooding ship. I can hear His heart beating with such intensity that it feels as though it could bust through His rib cage. I can feel His joy, and I can see His laughter. I can hear Him crying loudly, "My sons and daughters have come home!" I can see the party; the wine, the dancing, and the celebration. I can sense the Father's pride as He watches His children rejoice – He's biting His lip, exerting strenuous effort. He's seconds away from wailing uncontrollably with exuberant joy.

But outside the party, is an older brother. He's not happy. He feels cheated.

The Father approaches him and invites him to join the party.

No matter what side of the coin you fall on, know this, this party is for you.

From this moment on you won't have to work for God's love and supernatural power. You will live from a place of love and power that has been made possible through the finished work of Christ Jesus. You have been given permission to follow Jesus, to experience Jesus, and to reveal Jesus. The Holy Spirit has summoned you into His presence; the veil can no longer keep you away, for it has been torn by the hands of God.

IN CLOSING

YOU WERE BORN FOR THIS DAY.

You were given a voice. You don't need validation from a man when you have received validation from your Heavenly Father. You have a story that is powerful. You have an anointing that is extraordinary. You were not born to live a predictable life. You were created to redefine normal.

You are awesome, so be awesome. Make amazing things look boring. People will seek you for your perspective, and you will no longer fall for chicken height perspectives. You will no longer be overwhelmed by crisis, but you will overwhelm crisis with faith, hope, and love. You have been called by God to bum out pessimists. Your faith will cause the realists to humble themselves and repent. May your podium be in public, in sanctuaries without walls or pews. May your cell phone be your microphone that broadcasts the Gospel to the nations.

Don't back down, don't turn around, and don't shut up. Just because the room is dark, doesn't mean it isn't full.

Ignite fear, and you'll sell a few books. Ignite hope, and you'll change the world. You were created for nothing less. Make epic look small. Engage in big conversations, and don't tolerate your small dreams.

Many are looking to the future, waiting for a hope to come. The minority are possessed with hope and influencing the present. Even though hopelessness sells, you're not allowed to buy it. What you have, the world wants: Christ in you, the hope of glory.

People may reject religion, they may reject methods and tradition, but they will not reject hope. Their lips are parched, and their mouths are dry. The anthem of this world mirrors the cry of David in Psalm 42, "As the deer pants for the water so my soul starves for you."

In a moment you will close this book like you have done with hundreds of others. I hope that I have agitated your faith muscle. I hope that it spasms until you put it to work. I pray that you will view crisis differently from now on, and that you will see it as an opportunity to run into the phone booth and come out a hero. Spiderman's uncle Ben once said, "Peter, with great power, comes great responsibility." Uncle Ben was correct. You have a responsibility to engage, to go all in, and withhold nothing.

The world is looking for a hero, and Jesus has sent them you. You've been synced up with the Holy Trinity. There's the Father, the Son, and the Holy Spirit, and then there's you. They want to do some cool stuff with you.

You've been called to be a mover, a shaker, disrupter, a rumbler; a supernaturalist!

You've got what it takes. Now take down a giant, build up an ancient ruin, gather the scattered, and bind the brokenhearted.

If not you, then who?

If not now, then when?

Now go.

ACKNOWLEDGEMENTS

Thank you to all our team at Seattle Revival Center. I am so thankful to work with such creative, passionate and generous leaders. A special thanks to Jessica Daley and my mom, Debbie Webb, for editing this project. Thank you to my wife Andrea who is the real superhero in our home. She has been a bulletproof supermom and superwife through the unpredictable change associated with extended revival meetings, and dealing with me, as I act like a hermit in my study, writing while eating hundreds of pounds of dark chocolate. You are my inspiration, my accountability and my queen. I LOVE YOU!

Thank you to Bobby Conner for seeing something in me. Thank you Patricia King for believing in me. Thank you Leif Hetland for being so kind to me and sitting through my session (when you could have been watching TV back at your hotel) and then proceeding to shower me with such humbling words of affection. Thank you Charlie Shamp for not leaving. Thank you mom and dad, Jesus, and Pastor Gail for never giving up on me.

Thank you to **YOU** for buying this book *AND* actually reading it.

Now go, and be a pattern interrupt.

ABOUT THE AUTHOR

DARREN STOTT is the lead pastor at Seattle Revival Center, and the founder of Supernaturalist Ministries. He began pastoring at the age of 27 and is the author of Pattern Interrupt: *Dismantle Defeat, Overcome Ordinary, and Become a Rumbler.* In 2016, Darren and his leadership team experienced a Holy Ghost pattern interrupt; the church hosted a prophetic conference, and it didn't end. They found themselves thrusted by the West Coast Rumble into a revival in Seattle that they call The Apple Wine Awakening.

Darren's passion is to see people unstuck; to see the restorative and supernatural power of God invade every area of life and culture. Darren walks in power and revelation! He ministers out of the overflow; you never know what God is going to say or do through him!

AUTHOR CONTACT INFORMATION

E-mail: darrenstott@seattlerevivalcenter.com

Twitter / Periscope: @theDarrenStott

For publicity information:

Jeannette Wuhrman at (425) 228-0810

Jeannette@seattlerevivalcenter.com

STAY CONNECTED WITH DARREN AT:

Facebook.com/iSupernaturalist

www.iSupernaturalist.com

www.seattlerevivalcenter.com

www.srclive.com

36566126R00123

Made in the USA
San Bernardino, CA
26 July 2016